INCREDIBLE TODDLERS:
A Guide and Journal of Your Toddler's Discoveries

Promoting Toddlers' Safety and their Social, Emotional and Language Development

Incredible Toddlers

A GUIDE AND JOURNAL OF YOUR TODDLER'S DISCOVERIES

Promoting Toddlers' Safety and their
Social, Emotional and Language Development

CAROLYN WEBSTER-STRATTON, PH.D.

Incredible Toddlers
A Guide and Journal of Your Toddler's Discoveries
Promoting Toddlers' Safety and their Social, Emotional and Language Development

Book design by Janice St. Marie

Webster-Stratton, Carolyn
Incredible Toddlers

Includes bibliographical references.
ISBN 978-1-892222-08-4

Publisher:
Incredible Years, Inc.
1411 8th Avenue West
Seattle, WA 98119 USA
206-285-7565
www.incredibleyears.com

Printed in USA

CONTENTS

Chapter 2

Chapter 3
Coaching Toddlers' Social and Emotional Competence   *127*

Chapter 4

Positive Attention, Encouragement & Praise   175

Chapter 5
Separations, Reunions, Bedtime, and Routines   231

Chapter 6

Positive Discipline and Effective Limit Setting   279

Chapter 7
Positive Discipline—Handling Misbehavior   327

Chapter 8
Summary—Putting it All Together   379

Acknowledgments

First, I am grateful to all those parents and children who have participated in my research over the past 30 years. I have had the privilege of working closely with over 1000 parents who have shared with me their thoughts, feelings and experiences parenting their young children. Some parents were struggling to provide the most control, nurturing and predictable routines they could under very stressful environmental and poverty situations. Other parents were trying to figure out the best ways to respond to children who had behavior problems, ADHD and development delays. All were looking for support from others. Without these parents' input and commitment to helping their children be successful, my studies could not have been done and this book would not be possible.

Second, I am grateful to the many collaborators, coauthors and Parenting Clinic staff at the University of Washington who have worked with me over these many years to evaluate these Incredible Years parenting programs as well as to help to deliver them to groups of parents. There are now a cadre of accredited Incredible Years mentors and group leaders in many countries around the world who have joined me in this commitment to support parents by leading Incredible Years parent groups, helping them build their own support groups and to assure children get the best parenting possible. I am very honored by their dedication to this work and for all they are doing for their own communities. I am especially thankful to Stephen Scott in England, Judy Hutchings in Wales and Willy-Tore Mørch in Norway who have spear-headed research projects to evaluate these programs in their countries. They have inspired many professionals in their countries to support parents.

In Seattle, Jamila Reid has been my friend and colleague in my research and clinical work for the past 12 years and she has read, commented upon and edited drafts of this book, and I am very grateful for her wisdom and insights. Lisa St. George, director of Incredible Years business has helped make this book a reality by prodding me, proof-reading, copy editing, working with the graphic designer, and providing unfailing support. Much appreciation also goes to Janice St. Marie whose graphic design and collaboration has made this a fun book to read.

Third, I end by acknowledging my family. My own parents taught me a great deal about commitment, caring, and consistency. In particular, they have taught me about persistence—while my high school teachers seemed convinced I would never make it to college, my mother kept telling me nothing was meant to be easy and if I worked hard I could do anything. It is this cognitive message that undoubtedly has sustained me in my work and led to my belief that families can make the changes they want, especially if they have support from others. And as I have watched my own children, Seth and Anna, now in their 20's develop, explore and persist with their goals to help families, I dedicate this to them and all others who work to care about and support families and their children. Finally, I thank my husband, who remains my anchor and supports my work with families.

Foreword

Past History of Incredible Years Parenting Research

As a doctoral student I began to evaluate the effectiveness of the BASIC Incredible Years Video-based Parenting Programs in 1979 as part of my doctoral dissertation in educational psychology. Then as a researcher and professor at the University of Washington, I started the Parenting Clinic and subsequently conducted 6 randomized control group studies with parents of preschool children ages 3-6 years who had conduct problems. The objective was to help parents promote their children's social and emotional competence and reduce their aggression. Later I developed another parenting program to address the early school age period when such children are coping with school failure and underachievement. The objective of the school age program was to help parents support their children's academic success and partnerships with teachers as well as to learn how to teach their children problem solving strategies and how to make good friends. Over the next two decades our research team was able to demonstrate how positive and nurturing parenting and teaching and proactive discipline, and a social and emotional curriculum used with high-risk populations could promote children's self-regulation, social competence and problem solving skills as well as increase their school readiness and reduce their behavior problems. We conducted treatment studies for both parents and teachers who were helping children with conduct problems and ADHD as well as prevention studies for higher risk populations.

Current Objectives

In the past decade I have focused my attention on trying to develop programs for high risk parents of babies and toddlers because of the research showing how responsive and nurturing parenting responses make a powerful difference in promoting babies' and young children's optimal brain development. The goal is to offer support to parents and their children as early as possible in order to prevent later social, emotional, and behavioral problems from developing.

I separated out the Incredible Years Toddler Program from the original Preschool Program in 2007 because of the difference in the developmental milestones for these stages of development that require different understanding and discipline responses from parents and day care providers. Research regarding the Incredible Years Toddler, Preschool and School Age Programs can be found in the library on the Incredible Years web site, www.incredibleyears.com.

Toddler Development

Toddlers are incredible learners with an enormous, intrinsic capacity and curiosity to learn. Brain research seems to be confirming the early work of Piaget, a famous developmental psychologist who has described the stages and the qualitative changes in children's thinking processes. Both Piaget and the new brain research indicate that children seem to be best able to handle certain information at certain stages in their development. Information that is presented too early or too late in development is not learned as well as information that is presented during a critical learning period. By two to three or years of age toddlers are thought to have the largest number of neuron synapses possible, many more than adults have. Over subsequent years some of these neuron synapses will be strengthened while others are weakened. Research has indicated that the sculpting of this brain architecture will be highly influenced by parental social interactional responses. Indeed parents are children's first and best teachers. While parents can't change the genes or particular temperament their baby arrives with at birth, it is clear that children's brain wiring, circuitry, and eventual social, emotional, and academic competence is profoundly influenced by the way parents interact with them. Brain development seems to be a product of the "use it or lose it" principle; that is, neuron connections are strengthened by repetitive use and consistent nurturing responses from parents and disappear when they are not used or responded to.

Toddlers are driven with curiosity to explore, to examine and to investigate. Because of their limited language skills, imperfect physical skills, poor self-regulation emotion skills, they are impulsive, have difficulty stopping or slowing down when engaged in action, are physically aggressive and are easily distracted, making it difficult for them pay attention or listen when parents make a request. They are almost oblivious to the dangers that surround them and are intrigued with testing the limits of parental rules and safety. During the toddler stage parents are helping their children to successfully accomplish three developmental milestones: (1) secure bonding or attachment in their relationship with parents; (2) development of language, emotional and social expression; and (3) becoming more independent and developing a positive sense of self.

It is clear that these milestones need to be accomplished before children can proceed to learn skills during the preschool stage of development which involve: language fluency, pre-writing and pre-reading skills and how to follow adult's directions; emotional regulation such as ability to wait and accept limits; and social and friendship skills.

One might think of a toddler parenting pyramid providing necessary nutrients to children similar to the traditional food pyramid. Remember in the food pyramid, those items at the bottom of the pyramid such as grains, fruits, and vegetables, are considered essential foods. To stay healthy, you should eat lots of these foods each day. On the other hand, those foods at the top of the pyramid are to be used sparingly. Just as it is important to a balanced diet to eat a combination of foods in differing amounts, effective parenting involves using some strategies liberally and others in moderation. The foundation of the toddler parenting pyramid involves big and consistent doses of love, caring, child-centered play, positive talking, and responsive coaching interactions. This nurturing is the foundational soil and fertilizer needed to nurture your children's emotional, social and academic development. Like the child without essential foods each day, children without essential nurturing in their relationship with their parent will fail to grow or to develop healthy relationships. At the top of the parenting pyramid are other essential parenting tools, such as discipline and limit setting. These, too, are needed for healthy child development and to keep toddlers safe, but need to be used calmly, thoughtfully, and less frequently.

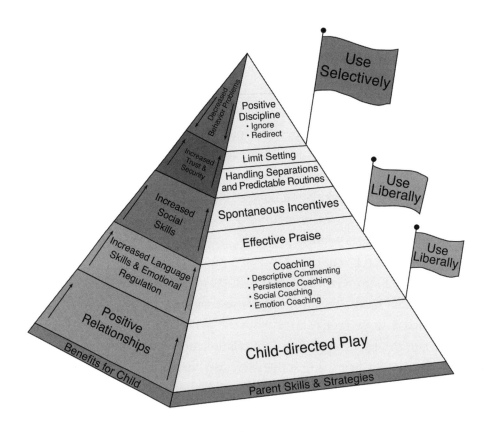

Parenting Pyramid Toddlers (1-3 years)

In this book I will discuss how toddlers' key developmental milestones involve an intense drive for further active exploration, autonomy, discovery of unique self, safe and secure relationship with parents, and social and language development. I will talk about ways parents can coach and strengthen their toddlers' cognitive, social, and emotional brain neuron connections and assure their toddlers' safety and healthy sleep patterns. Social skills and self-regulation are not innately programmed in children; rather children must be encouraged, prompted, and supported in their persistence at holding a crayon or spoon, efforts to put on their shoes, or using words to get what they want instead of grabbing or hitting. Parents will learn how to prune away toddlers' primitive aggressive physical responses and replace them with more prosocial behaviors by helping them use words to express how they feel and to recognize feelings in others. Parents will learn proactive discipline responses they can use when toddlers throw tantrums, cry, hit, or refuse to listen to or accept parental limits. In toddlers, these challenging behaviors are a normal developmental response that results when their drive for exploration and autonomy is confronted with parental limits. Toddlers are often frustrated by their limited ability to express themselves, their physical inabilities, and their lack of cognitive understanding. Parents will learn about toddlers' brain development from one to three years at this age and how they can join, support and nurture them in their incredible and individual exploration and adventure.

Each chapter has a journal section where parents can keep track of things their toddlers have learned to do each month as well as capture their memories of their toddlers' likes and dislikes and their favorite activities, songs, stories, and daily routines. I hope that this journal will be something you can share with other family members and care givers to let them know about your toddler's needs and personality. Perhaps when your toddler is older this will be something you can read and share with him or her. The time of toddlerhood passes much more quickly than you can imagine. When you are in the midst of constantly monitoring your toddler's safety and responding to a whirlwind of activity, it may seem like you will never have a relaxed meal again without a spill or a moment to yourself, but soon you will have a more independent preschooler who can get dressed, use the toilet, and entertain herself for longer periods of time. You will one day miss this time with your toddler and capturing some of it in this journal can help preserve its memory.

CHAPTER 1

Toddler-Directed Play Promotes Positive Relationships

Introduction

Toddlers' Developmental Journey

In the first year of life babies make an incredible developmental journey as they move from watching and observing parental responses, to six months of age where they are modeling or imitating their parents' reactions, to eventually discovering what their bodies can do as they become more mobile. In the second six months of life babies begin to crack the code of language, moving on from cooing at three months, to babbling at seven months. By one year your toddler is beginning to understand a great deal of your communication and may even be starting to produce a word or two.

At one year of age, as babies change from infants to toddlers, there is a shift in the way they interact with their parents. Suddenly, instead of just you and your baby in a cocoon of romance, your baby becomes aware of himself as an individual, what his body is capable of doing, and aware of other fascinating and irresistible objects in his environment. Telephones, kitchen drawers, dogs, drawers, purses, light sockets, and bookshelves become objects of both desire and danger. Toddlers who have developed a sense of trust in their environments feel that it is safe to explore and are almost oblivious to the dangers that surround them. They are driven with curiosity to examine and investigate and are often most drawn to forbidden objects. They are intrigued with testing the limits of parental rules and safety, and may playfully pull a dog's tail or fiddle with an electrical outlet while watching for their parents' response. Their physical skills are still imperfect and they may have difficulty with balance, or slowing down and stopping when engaged in action, or paying attention and listening when you make a request. This stage is alternately endearing, entertaining, exhausting, and exasperating for parents! And keeping your toddler safe is a full time job.

During the toddler stage parents will be helping their children successfully accomplish three developmental milestones:

Toddler Developmental Milestones
- Milestone One: secure bonding or attachment in their relationship with parents.
- Milestone Two: development of language, emotional and social expression.
- Milestone Three: to become more autonomous and develop a sense of self.

The parenting pyramid (see picture in foreward) helps explain some of the topics this book will cover to successfully help toddlers achieve these developmental milestones. This pyramid is similar to the traditional food pyramid. Remember in the food

Your baby becomes aware of himself as an individual, what his body is capable of doing, and aware of other fascinating and irresistible objects in his environment.

Positive and sensitive interactions

pyramid, those items at the bottom of the pyramid such as grains, fruits, and vegetables, are considered essential foods. To stay healthy, you should eat lots of these foods each day. On the other hand, those foods at the top of the pyramid are to be used sparingly. Just as it is important to a balanced diet to eat a combination of foods in differing amounts, effective parenting involves using some strategies liberally and others in moderation. The most important part of parenting is building a strong foundation of positive and sensitive interactions with your child. This foundation involves big and consistent doses of love, caring, child-centered play, positive talking, and coaching interactions. This nurturing on the part of parents is essential at all ages and stages of children's development from infancy, through the toddler and preschool years and into the school age years. This nurturing is the foundational soil and fertilizer needed to nurture your children's emotional, social and academic brain development. Playing and responsive talking with your children are key to promoting lasting attachments and positive relationships with them. Like the child without essential foods each day, children without essential nurturing in their relationship with their parent will fail to grow or to develop healthy relationships.

> The most important part of parenting is building a strong foundation of positive and sensitive interactions with your child.

Incredible parents nurture their children's growth

The Value of Play

The foundation of the parenting pyramid described above is devoted to toddler-directed play. There is a pervasive feeling today that when young children are playing, they are wasting time and doing something unimportant. Indeed, it is hard to break loose from the idea that play is frivolous, particularly in a society that puts such tremendous emphasis on academic goals, economic success, and work. However, play with parents is perhaps the most important aspect of a young child's life. Through regular, sensitive and responsive parent-toddler play interactions, the child develops a trusting emotional bond and important physical, cognitive, and social-emotional skills. These are all invaluable building blocks that provide the foundation for brain development. Research has indicated that babies come to us with the full complement of neurons but spend the first years of their

Play with parents is perhaps the most important aspect of a young child's life.

life developing new neuron connections. In fact, by age three, children will have double or triple the number of neuron connections that they had at birth. After that, the process of brain development involves pruning away those connections which are not being used and strengthening others. So, in the years between one and three, you play an important role in building important neuron connections in your toddler's brain.

Physical Play

The first and most obvious skills learned through play are physical. Play offers all kinds of opportunities for running, jumping, stretching, lifting, carrying, reaching, placing, and balancing. Physical play makes a positive contribution to your child's health and large muscle development, and improves your child's small muscle control and eye-hand coordination. Physical exercise is also good for fostering opportunities to strengthen vital connections in your toddler's growing brain. Did you know that fine motor skills such as gestures are thought to be related to speech skills and use the same brain neural circuits? This suggests that as fine-motor skills improve so does language skill.

Physical play makes a positive contribution to your child's health and large muscle development, and improves your child's small muscle control and eye-hand coordination.

Manipulative and Exploratory Play

This type of play involves curiosity, manipulating, exploring, problem solving, and gaining control over the activity. It also enhances the development of perceptual motor skills. Even the simplest toys permit the toddler to explore the dimensions of space, to manipulate, combine, and reassemble shapes, to create new forms, and to become sensitive to the color and texture of materials. Perhaps most importantly, your toddler learns that he or she can control the process and outcome of the entire activity. This is important for encouraging your toddler's developmental urge to explore and investigate and to be more independent.

Explore and investigate

Social Play

Toddlers engage in something called "parallel play"; that is, a child may play next to another child but often appears unaware of what his peer is doing. Although the children are playing next to each other, each is in his own play universe! In parallel play, the child does not initiate interactions with the other child and is not capable of waiting, taking turns, sharing, or cooperating. This is normal play for toddlers, and they are actually more aware of the other child than they appear to be. As toddlers become preschoolers, they begin to become more interactive with peers and more motivated to initiate interactions. However, this progression from parallel play to social play develops differently and at different rates in each child according to their brain development of language, social skills, emotional regulation and self-control.

It is noteworthy that the concept of playing games with clearly defined rules is not understood by children until ages six or seven years. Even preschoolers have difficulty with the concept of understanding permanent rules because they are still confusing fantasy and reality.

TODDLER ALERT

Jean Piaget, a giant in the field of child development psychology and intellectual development, has described developmental stages or steps in children's cognitive learning and understanding. He has shown that children are capable of handling certain information only at certain stages in development. For example, toddlers are not capable of understanding rules in games, so don't worry about this, it is normal.

Symbolic or Make-Believe Play

This type of play involves manipulating symbols, ideas and thoughts rather than people or objects. In make-believe play, children work with representations of things in their mind instead of the things themselves. Children may begin to engage in symbolic play as early as 18 months of age, and it is found in most three-year-old children. Imaginary companions or other indications of a rich fantasy life are typical of four year olds. Fantasy play steadily increases through middle childhood and then slowly begins to disappear.

Some adults and parents feel that pretend play and the creation of fantasy worlds and imaginary friends are bad for the mental health of children; others consider this type of play to be a sign of emotional disturbance. The evidence, however, indicates that just the opposite is true. Make-believe play is important for brain development. It is an opportunity for children to think symbolically, and it gives them a useful defense so they can work things out for themselves. It helps children get a better idea of what is real and what is not. The role playing that takes place while children are pretending is a good way for them to experience the feelings and emotions of others,

Thinking symbolically

and to learn how to be sensitive to the impact their actions have on the people around them. Thus it eventually helps them to become more empathic to another's perspective. Finally, research suggests that many of the most successful artists and scientists engaged in a lot of pretend play as young children.

For the child, play is not frivolous—it is an opportunity for physical, social and emotional brain nervous system development in almost every area. However, these benefits are not achieved without the critical involvement of parents in responsive, consistent and sensitive play interactions with their children.

Why Should Parents Play with Children?

Studies indicate that children have fewer behavior problems when parents play with them regularly.

Some parents believe that children have a natural predisposition toward play, and that children will automatically learn how to play if they are given the right toys. They believe play is "instinctual," that it is the one thing children can do for themselves. Some also assume that it is not necessary for adults to participate in play activities because peers satisfy children's play needs. However, research indicates that while children do engage in a certain amount of spontaneous play, it is not true  that children play by instinct. In fact, children have to learn how to play cooperatively, and unless there is some responsive, joyful parental play interactions, nurturing and coaching, children's creative or imaginary play will slowly disappear and peer play may become aggressive and conflictual! It has also been shown that children derive certain unique benefits from playing with their parents, especially when parents are being child-directed in play and are coaching specific social, emotional, and academic skills and behaviors. During child-directed play interactions, parents can coach their children to learn social skills, improve problem-solving skills, foster vocabulary, promote feelings communication, show approval for creativity and imagination, strengthen parent-child attachment, build self-esteem, and encourage persistence with a difficult activity. Studies have demonstrated that children tend to be more creative and have fewer behavior problems when parents and other adults engage in make-believe, child-directed play and coaching with them when they are young.

Barriers: What Stops Parents from Playing with Children?

There are many things that stop parents from playing with children. Some parents feel uncomfortable when they play with children and are not sure how to play with them. "After all," they say, "my parents didn't play with me, I turned out okay, why should I play with my child?" Whether they are parents or teachers, adults are often reluctant or embarrassed to participate in imaginary play, to crawl on the floor making train noises, to use puppets, or to act out fairy tales with young children. Other times parents feel too tired to engage in the intense interaction that toddler or preschooler play demands, or they may be bored by the repetitive games that fascinate young children. Still other parents find their toddler to be hyperactive, inattentive, defiant and aggressive during play and therefore don't find the play pleasurable. Finally, many parents don't realize that time spent playing with their child in responsive and sensitive ways is the most important gift they can give their child because it strengthens their child's social, emotional and cognitive brain architecture and maximizes their potential.

Adults are often reluctant or embarrassed to participate in imaginary play, to crawl on the floor making train noises, to use puppets, or to act out fairy tales with young children.

My playing presence with my child is a present

Are Some Types of Play Less Effective than Others?

Learn how to play

Parents often feel when they are playing with their children that they must supervise them and give them structured lessons or direct teaching on the rules for a game, or how to build the castle the "right" way, or how to draw a person with all the correct body parts. Other times parents enter into a competitive relationship with their children during play with the goal of teaching them to cope with "real life" interactions and to learn how to lose. These parents have the best intentions, but are actually engaging in types of play that may stifle creativity and problem solving ability, lead to children's frustration, resistance and less security in their relationship, and decrease their motivation to persist at challenging new tasks for fear of failure.

Does this Mean I Don't Know How to Play with my Child?

No! You are probably playing with your child in many effective ways, for parents are born to make a difference and have an impact. Above all else, young children need your attention, sensitivity, and loving interactions. However, there are ways that you can enhance your play times with your child that will lead to benefits for both of you! This kind of toddler-directed coaching is not something that comes naturally to many parents, and with the exception of play therapists, most adults have not been exposed to this type of play. The next three chapters will offer some pointers how to play more effectively and positively with children and how to avoid some of the common pitfalls that many parents encounter when playing with their toddler.

Above all else, young children need your attention, sensitivity, and loving interactions.

Enhancing play times

Expressing Joy with Your Toddler

Smiling and laughing

In the first months of life babies are intensively observing and mentally copying and recording their parents' smiles and joyful interactions. Babies can read emotions on parents' faces, even if they can't understand their language or words. This positive feedback, joyful expression and appreciation from parents contributes to the continued development of strong bonding and attachment between the toddler and his parents, as well as teaching toddlers about joy and trust in their relationships. The results of these positive relationships will be evident in the child's mood, behavior, and interactions with others. At the same time, these early experiences are contributing to social and emotional brain development and strengthening connections between neurons that will last forever.

Babies can read emotions on parents' faces, even if they can't understand their language or words.

When you are playing with your toddler, remember to show your joy and appreciation, get eye contact and say "thank you" when your toddler hands you a toy or involves you in his play. By doing this you are "modeling" important social skills you want to see your child imitate such as saying "thank you" or sharing and taking turns. This game of expressing gratitude and enthusiasm when your toddler initiates something with you is beginning to teach your toddler about social relations. Don't be surprised if your toddler wants you to repeat this sequence over and over again! Your child will delight in the predictability of giving you something, getting your eye contact, seeing your pleasure, hearing you say "thank you," and will be eager to see if he can make you do it again! What feels boring and repetitive to you is exciting and empowering for your child. This observational learning is how social behavior is learned. Your enthusiasm paired with modeling the same social behavior over and over again repetitively is teaching your toddler the behavior, building up a bank account of positive feelings, and forming his early memories and sense of self. All three toddler developmental milestones of bonding, social expression and sense of self are being supported by your simple and joyful interactions.

Singing love songs and rhymes

Singing

During the baby years, you probably were singing a lot to your baby and perhaps you noticed how this could calm his cries. During the toddler years singing is still a powerful way to strengthen your relationship as well as your toddler's language development. Now you can begin to try to encourage your toddler to sing as well. You can begin this by giving your toddler a chance to choose the song he wants to sing–thus giving him a sense of autonomy and independence. You will probably also find your toddler wants the same song to be repeated countless times. While it might seem boring to you to keep repeating the same song over and over, it isn't boring to your child. This repetition is important because every time you sing the song, your toddler is memorizing the words and gaining mastery over them. Toddlers particularly like songs with motions and silly sounds. The key to toddlers' learning is repetition, movement and predictability because it helps them feel mastery, confidence and secure.

While it might seem boring to you to keep repeating the same song over and over, it isn't boring to your child.

Pretend Play

During play times parents can foster the beginning stages of pretend or imaginary play with their toddlers, although complex imaginary worlds won't emerge until children are three years and older.

You can do this by assembling a box of old clothes, hats, and shoes to encourage your toddler's dress up play and make believe. Other household items such as pots and pans, Cheerios, wooden spoons and water will also encourage make believe cooking and eating. Small hand puppets, pretend or old telephones, baby strollers, and other household objects are particularly helpful for two- to three-year-olds because they encourage imaginary play and use of language skills. While imaginary play in toddlers is just beginning to emerge, as it develops it will encourage your toddler to speak, to act out social skills and to express feelings. You will likely see your child's imaginary play imitating his or her own life experience. At this age children like to pretend to feed, bathe, and dress their stuffed animals or pretend to vacuum the house, mow the lawn, or wash the dishes.

Being playful

Engaging in pretend play with your toddler contributes to building a positive relationship with you, and promotes his language development, creative thinking, story-telling ability, empathy, and perspective taking. It helps children learn about regulating emotions and sharing feelings. Research has indicated that children who engage in imaginary play have a greater capacity to understand others' emotions, are more empathic, and have fewer behavior problems.

When you are playing with your toddler, you can pretend by making the sound of the animal, or truck, or plane as your child plays with the objects. You can take small action figures or hand puppets and use them to speak to your child by asking such things as, "Can I play with you?" or, "My horse is thirsty, can he have some of your water?" Probably playing house and making forts is something enjoyable many of us remember from our childhoods. Allow tables and chairs to become houses and palaces, and doll figures to turn into friends or relatives. It is especially fun for children when parents engage in this imaginary play with them.

Remember that pretend play at the toddler age is in its infancy of development and usually doesn't involve others.

Normally toddlers play side by side in "parallel play" with little awareness of the child next to them. However, you can help your child be aware of the presence of yourself or another child playing with them by prompting them to notice what someone else is doing. For example, you might say, "Mary is sitting next to you building a really tall tower." "You and I are both playing with these dolls together." "Ben is

Research has indicated that children who engage in imaginary play have a greater capacity to understand others' emotions.

Imaginary play

looking for a blue block for his garage." You can prompt or suggest to your child that he share or help you or a friend. "I'd like to use one of those spoons. Could you share one with me?" "Can you help Ben find that blue block?" If your child responds, you can use a labeled praise: "You shared that spoon with me. That was a friendly thing to do." "Ben looks happy that you helped him find that block." In this way you are helping your child be aware of how he can appropriately initiate an interaction with a friend. If your child doesn't respond to your prompts, don't force him to interact or to share. He may not be developmentally ready for this step, and if you insist, you may be met with resistance.

If your child doesn't respond to your prompts, don't force him to interact or to share.

Be Toddler-Directed or Child-Centered

Child-directed interactions

One of the essential aspects of successful parent-toddler play is to be able to be child-centered or toddler-directed which means following the lead or directions of your toddler. This is important because toddlers are driven to explore and are discovering their sense of self, the ability to control others and their autonomy. Therefore they need safe opportunities such as play times to exercise this independence and control. Remember that in a great deal of the rest of their lives they are being controlled by others.

Consider what happens when one mother is trying very hard to teach her two-year-old son, Darren, how to play tic-tac-toe. She imposes a lot of structure and tries to teach Darren the rules about how X's and O's are supposed to be played. Darren clearly does not understand the rules, or why they have to take turns, or why the O's have to go in a row. When Darren tries to take one of his mother's X's she replies, "No these are my X's you can't have these." When she tries harder to teach him the rules, he resists even more. By the end the mother feels frustrated and Darren walks away disliking the game. In this case, Darren's mother has positive intentions to try to teach him something, but she is being too parent-directed and not responding to the cues Darren is giving her that he is not developmentally ready to follow the rules of this game. Moreover, she is modeling being uncooperative (when she says "no these are my X's you can't have these"). So from this experience Darren is learning that he doesn't like this game, and that he shouldn't share the game pieces.

Instead, the first step in playing with children, is to follow their lead, ideas and imagination rather than imposing your own. If Darren's mother had allowed him

to be more autonomous and to manipulate the X's and O's, hang them on his ears or repeatedly fill and empty the box, he would have enjoyed this exploration process, developed a beginning interest in the game and enjoyed his playing time with his mother. She could have offered to share an X with him, and he might have shared one back. In this case she would follow Darren's lead to see what he wants to do with the X's and O's. Even if he just takes them out and puts them back in, this is a worthwhile activity because he is exploring and using his fine motor skills.

During child-directed play, try not to structure or organize activities for your child by giving commands or instructions. Don't try to teach anything. Instead, imitate your child's actions and do what he asks you to do. By responding positively to your child's ideas, you will find he is more involved and interested in play and will learn how to be cooperative by modeling your behaviors. Don't worry that your child will never learn rules to a structured game. Your child will actually let you know when he is ready for this stage of play. Sometime between the ages of 5-8 years old, most children will show an intense interest in the rules of games. In fact, at this stage they may become quite rigid about the rules, and at some point your child will probably remember the rules better than you do!

Some key play principles for children's effective learning:
- Make play and learning fun (the "fun principle"—children will repeat what is fun and interesting).
- Respond to your child's cues that he is interested and ready to learn.

> The first step in playing with children, is to follow their lead, ideas and imagination rather than imposing your own.

- Praise and support what your child is interested in doing (e.g., let child dangle circles on ears or fill and empty the box).
- Let your child set the rules of the game and model appropriate play skills, such as cooperating with your child's ideas, waiting a turn, and describing what he is doing that is appropriate. Children are not developmentally ready to understand rules of a game until they are 5–8 years old.
- Be flexible and avoid power struggles or competitive games.

Piaget, the Swiss scientist mentioned above, was interested in how children play, and how they learn rules. He watched children playing marbles and found that very few children have the concept that rules are permanent until they are seven to eight years of age. He noticed that young children frequently changed the rules, and that children played with each other using different sets of rules. Piaget described the concept of "reciprocity" in play, and stated that if adults went along with children's rules and provided a model of acceptance, children were more likely to go along with parents' rules in other situations.

Sometimes parents think children need to learn how to lose at games. This is not developmentally appropriate until children are early school age. Moreover, in life, young children often "lose" in the sense that they are made to do things that they don't want to. Think of the constant stream of rules and demands imposed on them for going to bed, eating, leaving the house at a certain time, or getting dressed. Play is the one opportunity where they can feel like they are winning and experience legitimate power and control.

Play is the one opportunity where toddlers can feel like they are winning and experience legitimate power and control.

Feeling like a winner

Choice of Toys

It is not necessary to have fancy toys for your play interactions. In fact, the simpler unstructured toys such as blocks are preferable because they allow your child to use his own imagination and creativity. Also, many household objects such as cereal boxes, pots and pans, a bucket of water, and Cheerios and a spoon can be wonderful toys for toddlers. Some of the old fashioned toys are still the best fun such as building blocks, dress up clothes, clumps of play dough, sand and water, or making a fort out of the living room furniture. Research shows that a child's brain grows and is stimulated by things the child is most interested in. So if your child likes drawing or big blocks, or water play, or trains, you'll be helping your child's brain development by finding ways to explore what he is most interested in. This is called "being child-directed."

The simpler unstructured toys such as blocks are preferable because they allow your child to use his own imagination.

Pace the Play to Suit Your Child

Toddlers tend to repeat the same activity over and over again. How often have you seen your toddler repeatedly fill and empty a box? How often have your groaned inwardly when asked to read the same story yet again? It can be tempting to quicken the pace by introducing some new idea or a more sophisticated way of using a toy. The problem is that children need to rehearse and practice an activity many times in order to master it. Think about how much repetition you need to learn a new language or master a golf swing. It takes time to feel confident. If toddlers are pushed into a new activity too quickly, they will feel incompetent or they may get frustrated and give up playing because the challenge is too great.

> If toddlers are pushed into a new activity too quickly, they will feel incompetent or they may get frustrated.

Be sure to pace the play to your child's tempo. Just as you were engaged in a back and forth recripocal dance with your baby, the same is true with toddlers. Give your child time to use his imagination and to think about what steps he wants to take next. Don't push him because you are bored. Be patient and wait until he decides to do something different and respond to his rhythm or pace. Remember children move much more slowly from one idea to another than adults. Pacing slowly will help you expand your child's attention span and encourage him to concentrate on one activity for a period of time.

Being an Appreciative Audience

It is important to be a good audience when you play with your toddler. Sometimes parents get so involved in the play that they ignore their children or take over what their children are doing. The toddler ends up watching the parents play. Remember Darren who got so frustrated because he didn't understand the rules of the tic-tac-toe? Other times parents are multi-tasking and trying to read, cook, or talk or text on the phone while they play. Your toddler is good at sensing when your mind is elsewhere—you may even notice him getting more demanding when you are only focusing half of your attention on him.

Protecting

When playing with your toddler, give him your undivided focused attention and positive support. Try to think of yourself as an appreciative audience and applaud what your child is doing without a lot of rules and restrictions getting in the way. Play is one of the few times that toddlers can have some control and autonomy as long as they are behaving appropriately. Sit back and watch what your toddler is doing and

praise his efforts. Some parents hesitate to praise or disturb a child when he is playing well because they believe their child will then demand more of their attention and the play activity will be disrupted. (They believe in the "let sleeping dogs lie principle".) It is true that when you first begin to give attention to your child's play, your child may seem to seek more attention. However, this is because your child has not yet determined that he can reliably expect your positive attention for his play rather than for inappropriate behavior. If you ignore your child's quiet play, it will soon disappear and your child will use inappropriate ways (loud screams) to receive attention from you.

Ending Play

Children's appetite for your attention is almost insatiable. Most toddlers would be happy if you played all day long. This can feel overwhelming. Make it your goal to give your child as much undivided playtime as you can, but don't feel guilty that you can't play as much as your child wants. If you set aside several short child-focused play times each day (even 10 minutes), you will be giving your child the message that when you are playing with him, you are really present for him. This may also buy you a little more freedom to do your own household tasks because children who can count on their parents' predictable attention each day will gradually learn to be more self directed at other times.

Ending play with your child can be difficult—but remember it is always a good sign if your child doesn't want to end play because that means he had a good time—and who wants to end something that is a lot of fun? It is important that you prepare your child for the end of play and give him some time to make the transition. You can use a timer or a bell or some music to warn your child that the playtime is almost up. If your child protests when you are done playing you can say, "I know, you're feeling sad that it's time for me to stop playing now. I had fun with you too. After dinner, we will have another chance to play." As your child learns that you are predictable and will play with him regularly it will be easier for him to accept the end of play. He will know and understand that you and he will have another chance to play again soon.

Self-directed play

Children who can count on their parents' predictable attention each day will gradually learn to be more self-directed.

Be Responsive to Your Toddler's Temperament

Every toddler has his or her own particular temperament and unique neurological adaptation to life experiences and complex individuality. Think about your toddler's temperament and way of interacting with the world. Is your toddler easy, slow to warm up, challenging, or some combination of these traits? Children with different temperaments will respond to their environments in different ways and one of your jobs as a parent is to try to be responsive to your child's individual temperamental needs. This may mean providing a shyer, withdrawn child with time and space to adjust to new situations, while also encouraging some risk-taking. Or this may mean providing a lot of room for movement and exploration for a very active child, while providing safe limits and encouraging calm behavior and self-regulation skills. Your child's temperament style is biological and innate, not something that is learned from parents. If you have a child with a more challenging temperament, don't blame yourself or your child. Your child is not purposely trying to be difficult or annoying. Respect your child's temperament and uniqueness. Complete the temperament behavioral style questionnaire at the end of this chapter and think about what temperament categorization applies to your toddler.

Regardless of your child's innate temperament, most toddlers will be demanding, physically active, curious and eager to explore their world, inattentive, easily distracted, and driven to assert their independence or autonomy. They may seem oppositional or defiant at times but these behaviors are normal expressions of their search for independence. The intensity of each of these characteristics will be variable and influenced by your child's basic temperament and your responses. When playing with your child try to consider your toddler's temperament, sensitivity, and

> Your child's temperament style is biological and innate, not something that is learned from parents.

Feeling understood

I respect my toddler's temperament

ability to sustain attention when planning activities that are most suitable for your child. Try to be realistic about your expectations for how long your activity may last before your child is on to something else or how difficult it will be for him to end play and give up your attention. If you have an intense toddler, you will need to strive to be tolerant, patient, and calm. If your child is very distractible, keep your instructions clear, tasks simple, and remove competing distractions when possible. Redirect your child without shame or anger and give lots of praise and encouragement for focused behavior.

If you have an intense toddler, you will need to strive to be tolerant, patient, and calm.

Toddler-Proofing

Toddlers have discovered they now have the physical skills as well as the curiosity, security, and intense hunger to explore their environment. They have few inhibitions or awareness of possible dangers that surround them. Indeed it is the rare toddler who has managed to get through these years without some bruises or falls. Parents need to be vigilant about keeping their toddler safe and most will say this is a full time job and easier said than done. You've spent the past year baby proofing your house for a baby who was not very mobile, and now you must make your house safe for a mobile toddler. To do this try to think like a curious, highly active two-year-old detective who sees adventures lurking around every corner. This means you have to ensure every room in your house is toddler-proofed. Please complete the toddler safety checklist at the end of this chapter and determine your goals.

Safe environment

To Sum Up...

The most obvious benefit of play is that it aids physical development. When toddlers walk, toddle, jump, yell, and laugh, it contributes to their good health and the development of gross motor skills as well as perceptual motor skills.

But even more so, toddler-directed play is a learning situation for children because it is an opportunity for them to learn who they are, what they can do, and how to socially relate to the world around them. Through play, toddlers are able to discover and explore, begin to use their language and imagination, and test out ideas. Through these toddler-directed play experiences, children gradually learn how to gain control over their environment, and they become more autonomous and self-confident. How often have you heard a child proudly say, "See what I did?" Play allows children to push the limits in a positive way; to extend what they've learned as far as they can. It gives children the freedom to fail and make mistakes and to learn from them, and the opportunity to explore the limits of their skills.

Play is also a means of emotional expression. Children live in a world where they have little power and few legitimate opportunities to express emotions such as anger, dependency, or insecurity. Fantasy play can reduce children's feelings of fear, anger, and inadequacy, and provides experiences that enhance children's feelings of enjoyment, control, and success. When children try out roles such as being mother, father, aunt, teacher, or doctor, they have an opportunity to see the world from other points of view. This cognitive process helps them become less egocentric and more empathic towards others. Through

Through play, toddlers are able to discover and explore, begin to use their language and imagination, and test out ideas.

play, children can communicate their thoughts, needs, satisfactions, problems, and feelings. A parent can learn a lot about their child's feelings by watching, listening to, and engaging in pretend play with their child.

Finally, when children play in a supportive, child-directive environment with their parents, they can be creative. They are free to try out their imagination, exploring the impossible and the absurd, and developing confidence in the value of their thoughts and ideas. During make-believe play, boxes, blocks, and articles of furniture can become houses, palaces, or entire kingdoms; doll figures can turn into mothers, children, and even monsters. Play develops the basic skills for social interaction. Children learn how to cooperate, share, and be sensitive to the feelings of others through their play interactions with parents.

Thus for the child, play is not frivolous—it provides an opportunity for brain growth and development in almost every area. However, it takes the involvement of parents in nurturing and responsive play interactions for children to feel safe, to develop a positive sense of self, and a healthy social and emotional nervous system. It is critical for parents to devote time to supportive play activities by being toddler-directed, joyful, imaginative and to join in their child's imaginary mind in pretend play. This is one of the most intimate places you can be with your toddler.

Points to Remember about
TODDLER-DIRECTED PLAY

- Encourage your child's curiosity to explore new objects, settings & people.
- Follow your child's lead.
- Pace at your child's level.
- Don't expect too much—give your child time.
- Don't compete with your child.
- Don't focus on the "correct" way or specified rules for a game.
- Try not to ask questions, rather observe and respond to your child's initations.
- Model cooperation by doing what your child asks you to do.
- Praise and encourage your child's self-discovery and creativity; don't criticize.
- Engage in pretend and make-believe with your child.
- Be an attentive and appreciative audience.
- Give your toddler choices when possible.
- Allow your child to change his mind; be process oriented vs. product oriented.
- Curb your desire to give too much help—give just enough support to avoid frustration but not so much you take over your toddler's exploration.
- Reward quiet play with your attention.
- Laugh and have fun.

I follow my child's lead in play

I practice child-directed play

Points to Remember about
GOODNESS OF FIT—
MANAGING YOUR TODDLER'S TEMPERAMENT

Even if parents have different temperaments than their children, they can still strive for a good fit. A good fit is when parents' demands and expectations are compatible with their child's temperament, abilities and characteristics. The goal is always to manage and support rather than to squelch or change temperament.

Here are some tips for achieving a good fit and managing your toddler's temperament.

• Realize that your child's temperament style is not your "fault" because temperament is something biological and innate, not something that is learned from parents. Your child is probably not purposely trying to be difficult or irritating. Don't blame him or yourself.

• Respect your child's temperament without comparing to siblings or peers or trying to change his or her basic temperament.

• Consider your own basic temperament and behavior and tailor your parenting responses when they clash with your child's responses to encourage a better fit.

• Remember what you model for your children is what they learn from you.

• Try to consider and anticipate your child's adaptability, activity level, sensitivity, biological rhythms, and ability to sustain attention when planning activities that are most suitable for your child.

• Try to focus on the issues of the moment. Do not project into the future.

• Review your expectations for your child, your preferences and your values. Are they realistic and appropriate?

Avoid labeling your child

• Anticipate high risk situations and try to avoid or minimize them.

• Enjoy the interactions and the differences in each of your children.

• Avoid labeling your child as bad or difficult as this may lead to negative self-image and further compound his difficulties.

• Try to distinguish between a tantrum that is temperamentally induced (reaction to disappointment) versus one that is manipulative (designed to get parent to give in).

• Help your child develop a positive self-esteem.

• Find a way to get relief for yourself and your toddler by scheduling some time apart.

Remember, above all, temperament qualities can be shaped to work to a child's advantage if they are sensibly managed.

PHYSICAL DEVELOPMENTAL MILESTONES
12–18 MONTHS

- walk and cruise (12 months)
- holds out arm or leg to help with dressing (13-14 months)
- toddles well (14 -15 months)
- runs (15-16 months)
- increased hand movements–can turn pages of a book (16 months)
- enjoys climbing (16-17 months)
- stacks blocks (16-17 months)
- throws a ball (18 months)
- scribbles (18 months)

Increased finger dexterity

SOCIAL & EMOTIONAL DEVELOPMENTAL MILESTONES
12–18 MONTHS

- Gesture, point and babble (12 months)
- Wave bye-bye (10–12 months)
- Single word (12 months)
- Use two words (13 months)
- Enjoys looking at self in mirror (13–14 months)
- Holds out arm or leg to help with dressing (13–14 months)
- Combines gestures with words to make needs known (14 months)
- Imitates others (14 months)
- Initiates games (14–15 months)
- Responds to instructions (14–15 months)
- Uses spoon (14–15 months)
- Drinks from a cup with assistance (14 months)
- Uses three words (15 months)
- Adopts "no" as favorite word (15–16 months)
- Becomes attached to object such as a blanket (16 months)
- Switches from one to two naps (16–17 months)
- Uses some common consonants (t, d, n, w) (16 months)
- Uses six words regularly (17 months)

Combines gestures with words

- Enjoys pretend games (17 months)
- Enjoys music and dances to music (17 months)
- Says please and thank you (18 months)
- Uses two word combinations (18 months)
- Will look at pictures in a book, point to pictures and can turn pages on own (18 months)
- Responds to questions with pointing and sounds to indicate some conversation (18 months)
- Looks at object that parent points to rather than parent's finger (18 months)
- Understands about 100–150 words but cannot say them (18 months)
- Is immensely curious to examine objects (12–18 months)

I am learning the Toddler dance

ENSURING MY TODDLER'S SAFETY
Toddlerproofing Checklist: PART 1

Toddlers are driven to explore and are curious about everything–they have no inhibitions and don't understand danger! Therefore one of the biggest challenges for parents is doing as much as possible to keep your child safe. Do this checklist and see how toddler-proof you are.

Action	yes	no
Monitor and supervise my toddler at all times; am vigilant about this	☑	☐
Toddler-proofed every room in my house	☑	☐
Keep emergency numbers next to the phone (including a poison control center number)	☑	☐
Keep curtain and blind cords out of reach	☑	☐
Ensured all my windows are lockable and use window guards	☑	☐
Put plastic covers on electrical outlets	☐	☐
Unplug electrical appliances when not in use	☐	☐
Put latches on cupboard doors and drawers	☐	☐

Action	yes	no
Keep chairs and cribs away from windows	❑	❑
Keep small objects such as coins, marbles, batteries and purses out of reach of my toddler	❑	❑
Keep toilet seat closed at all times. If my toddler is attracted to water, keep the bathroom door closed/locked or use a toilet seat lock	❑	❑
When bathing child, I do not leave a filling/filled tub unattended. I keep my toddler with me while tub is filling. Once my child is in tub, I do not leave, even for a second. I drain water as soon as my child is out of bath	❑	❑
Do not leave my toddler alone with my pet and keep litter box in walled off area	❑	❑
Make sure my plants are not dangerous (called poison control center)	❑	❑
Install baby gates at the top and bottom of stairs	❑	❑
Use fire-retardant sleepwear	❑	❑
Turn down the temperature on my hot water heater	❑	❑

Action	yes	no
Lock all medications (including vitamins) in lockable medicine cabinet or cash box that can be stashed on a top shelf	❏	❏
Keep all products such as shampoo, cosmetics, nail polish remover, household cleaners, scissors, razors out of my toddler's reach	❏	❏
Keep electrical hair dryers out of my toddler's reach	❏	❏
Keep stuffed animals away from cooking area	❏	❏
Turn pot handles toward back of stove & secure oven door	❏	❏

My home is toddler-proofed

ENSURING MY TODDLER'S SAFETY
Toddlerproofing Checklist: PART 2

Now let's look at some more things to check when toddler proofing. After completing this make a goal for yourself for areas you need to safety proof.

Action	yes	no
Never leave my toddler unattended while eating; do not give him popcorn, peanuts, hot dog rounds, whole grapes, or other foods that could be easily stuck in the windpipe	❏	❏
Take a first aid and infant/toddler CPR class so that I know how to respond if my child is choking	❏	❏
Have a play area in kitchen–give him his own cupboard with plastic containers, wooden spoons etc.	❏	❏
Avoid latex balloons–stick to Mylar	❏	❏
Put fireplace guards around fireplaces or heaters	❏	❏
Supervise my toddler when he's using a riding toy	❏	❏
Use a helmet when my child is riding a tricycle (to get in habit)	❏	❏

Action	yes	no
Use a government-approved car seat. I never ride in the car with my toddler in my arms. Know the height and weight specifications for my child's car seat (children should be kept rear facing until they weigh at least 20lbs and are one year of age). Keep my toddler in a car seat until he is at least 40 lbs and then in a booster seat until he is 4'9". A five-point harness is safer than a shoulder belt	❑	❑
TV is not positioned in a place where it can topple over on my toddler	❑	❑
Never leave my child unattended in car, even if dashing to the store for a minute	❑	❑
Put sunscreen on and sun hats on my children when in the sun	❑	❑
Crib mattress is on lowest level so he can't tumble out and there are not large toys in crib which he can use to climb out of crib	❑	❑
Stay within arm's reach of my toddler near traffic, water, or other dangerous situations	❑	❑

I am vigilant about safety

Action	yes	no
Teaching my toddler to "stop" for traffic and to hold my hand as we cross the street, but I understand that he is too young to be relied upon to follow these directions consistently	❏	❏
In very dangerous or crowded situations (near water, near traffic, in a busy airport) I keep my toddler safe in a backpack, stroller or harness	❏	❏
When I buy toys I will check their safety rating	❏	❏

My home is a safe environment

My Toddler's Temperament

Here are that nine traits proposed by Thomas, Chess and Birch (1968) that describe a child's reactivity to his or her environment. Rate where your toddler is on each of these traits.

My toddler's activity level: *This is the amount s/he moves or wiggles or is on the go versus how much s/he relaxes or sits still or prefers quiet activities.*

VERY ACTIVE   QUIET AND RELAXED
1   2   3   4   5

The regularity of my toddler's bodily functions: *This is the predictability of his or her sleep times, appetite, and bowel movements.*

MOSTLY REGULAR/PREDICTABLE   MOSTLY IRREGULAR/UNPREDICTABLE
1   2   3   4   5

My toddler's adaptability: *This is how s/he adapts to changes in routine, new food, new people, or new places.*

ADAPTS QUICKLY   SLOW TO ADAPT
1   **2**   **3**   **4**   **5**

My toddler's approach: *This is how eager s/he is to try something new versus how fearful or shy s/he is when presented with a new situation or person.*

EAGER INITIAL APPROACH   INITIAL WITHDRAWAL OR RELUCTANCE
1   2   3   4   5

My toddler's physical sensitivity: *This is how sensitive s/he is to noise, tastes, textures, bright lights, touch or temperature.*

NOT SENSITIVE   VERY SENSITIVE

1   2   3   4   5

My toddler's intensity: *This is how intensely he or she reacts emotionally to things, even minor events.*

HIGH EMOTIONAL INTENSITY   MILD CALM REACTION

1   2   3   4   5

My toddler's distractibility: *This is the degree to which s/he is distracted by sounds, sights, or things in the environment versus how much s/he can shut out external stimuli and pay attention.*

VERY DISTRACTIBLE   NOT DISTRACTIBLE

1   2   3   4   5

My toddler's mood: *This is the degree to which s/he is happy or positive versus negative.*

POSITIVE MOOD   NEGATIVE MOOD

1   2   3   4   5

My toddler's persistence: *This is the degree to which s/he can persist or sustain his or her attention versus how easily s/he gives up in the face of obstacles.*

LONG ATTENTION SPAN   SHORT ATTENTION SPAN

1   2   3   4   5

Parents' Viewpoint
MY TEMPERAMENT FITS WITH MY TODDLER'S

Parents also have their own temperament and need to understand how their own temperament style meshes with their child's temperament. Sometimes parent-child temperaments are very similar; other times they are very different. Both similar and different parent-child temperaments may result in clashes or be complementary.

Complete the following temperament questionnaire for yourself. See what you find out about your temperament fit with your child. Think about how you can manage a good fit.

My activity level:
This is the amount I move versus how much I relax. I am:

VERY ACTIVE   QUIET AND RELAXED

1	2	3	4	5

The regularity of my bodily functions:
This is the predictability of my sleep times, eating, and bowel movements. I am:

MOSTLY REGULAR/PREDICTABLE   MOSTLY IRREGULAR/UNPREDICTABLE

1	2	3	4	5

My adaptability:
This is how I adapt to changes in routine, new food, new people, or new places. I usually:

ADAPTS QUICKLY   SLOW TO ADAPT

1	2	3	4	5

My approach:

This is how eager I am to try something new versus how fearful or shy I am. Usually I am:

EAGER INITIAL APPROACH   INITIAL WITHDRAWAL OR RELUCTANCE

1   2   3   4   5

My physical sensitivity:

This is my sensitivity to noise, textures, bright lights, temperature is:

NOT SENSITIVE   VERY SENSITIVE

1   2   3   4   5

My intensity:

This is the intensity of my reactions or emotions:

HIGH EMOTIONAL INTENSITY   MILD CALM REACTION

1   2   3   4   5

My distractibility:

This is the degree to which I am distracted and notice everything around me versus how much I can shut out external stimuli. Usually I am:

VERY DISTRACTIBLE   NOT DISTRACTIBLE

1   2   3   4   5

My mood:

This is the degree to which I am happy or positive versus negative. Usually I have a:

POSITIVE MOOD   NEGATIVE MOOD

1   2   3   4   5

My persistence:

This is degree to which I can persist or sustain my attention versus how easily I give up. Usually I have a:

LONG ATTENTION SPAN   SHORT ATTENTION SPAN

1   2   3   4   5

MY TODDLER'S PLAY JOURNAL

Write here some of your toddler's favorite toys, play activities and beginning steps toward pretend play.

Toddler's Viewpoint
THINGS I CAN DO (12–18 months)

Activity	Date	Observations/Comments
I can point at things		
I can wave bye bye		
I can say two words		
I like looking at myself in the mirror		
I can imitate adults		
I can use a spoon		
I can make my needs known with sign language		

Toddler's Viewpoint
THINGS I CAN DO (12–18 months)

Activity	Date	Observations/Comments
I like to play games such as hide and seek		
I like to push or pull a toy		
I respond to instructions		
I love to say "no"		
I am attached to _____ (blanket or stuffed animal)		
I am thinking about switching to one nap a day		
I can say 3-4 words now		

Toddler's Viewpoint
THINGS I CAN DO (12–18 months)

Activity	Date	Observations/Comments
I love pretend games		
I like to dance to music		
I like to look at pictures in a book		
I can turn pages now by myself		
If you point at something I will follow		
I understand quite a bit of what is said		
I can scribble		

Toddler's Viewpoint
THINGS I CAN DO (12–18 months)

Activity	Date	Observations/Comments
I am so curious		
I am cruising now		
I am learning how to run		
Wow I am starting to climb		
I can stack blocks –guess how many?		
I can throw a ball, try me!		

MY TODDLER'S PICTURE
(12–18 months)

CHAPTER 2

Promoting Toddlers' Pre-School Readiness With Academic and Persistence Coaching

Introduction

In chapter one we talked about how parents' child-directed, appreciative and focused attention on their toddlers' play helps build a positive feeling and strong bond between parents and children. Children feel valued by their parents when parents spend time with them, follow their lead, and show they enjoy being with them. In this chapter we will discuss ways parents can "coach" their children to build their language development skills, prepare them for preschool, and help them persist with a difficult learning activity even when frustrated. Preschool readiness implies that toddlers have made significant progress toward their developmental milestones including a strong bond or attachment with their parents, a sense of self and autonomy, and language, social and emotional expression. We will talk about two types of descriptive commenting:

Academic and Persistence Coaching which will foster your toddler's language development and her sustained attention span with play activities. Two more kinds of coaching related to social and emotional development will be discussed next in Chapter 3.

Descriptive commenting is really an expansion of the "parent-ese" language that parents use with their babies that involves a sing-song-like voice and exaggerated facial expressions and smiles, but now it takes on a somewhat more elaborate language form. Instead of single vowels or words spoken slowly in a high-pitched, melodious voice, your sentences gradually become longer, more detailed and complex. When your child was a baby you likely talked to her constantly, giving a running commentary on her activities while diapering, changing, and playing with her. This commentary often sounds like a sports announcer's play-by-play description of a game. For example, *"You're grabbing your toes! Let's put this wet diaper in the pail and get you a clean fresh diaper. I'm snapping it up. Now I'm sitting you up. There you're up!"* You will continue to do the same commenting with your toddler but expand your descriptions to increase your toddler's awareness of what she is seeing, doing, thinking or feeling. This is a novel way of communicating and parents often feel uncomfortable and artificial when they first try talking to their child in this way. This is merely the awkwardness anyone feels whenever attempting to do something unfamiliar. Remember your initial discomfort when you were learning to drive a car, play the piano, or some other new skill? The discomfort will diminish as you practice in a variety of situations. If you are persistent in learning to do this descriptive commenting, you will find that your child will come to love this kind of attention and her language skills will blossom.

TODDLER ALERT

Research shows that children whose parents talked to them frequently as babies and toddlers had higher IQs and richer vocabularies than children who heard less language.

From Consonants and Vowels to Babbles to Words and Combined Words

I mirror my toddler's word efforts

When all babies around the world are about a year old, they are babbling streams of consonants and vowels such as adabababa with their parents. After this verbal babbling stage is completed (usually between 12 and 18 months), children start to use the unique words of their own culture. A child's first single words are often nouns describing familiar people (mama, dada) or common and interesting objects (ball, baby, cat, water). At this age most children will also understand and follow simple directions, such as, "Please give me the toy." In English we typically hear 18-month to two-year-old children starting to use two word combinations to make sentences, such as "all gone" or "uh-oh!" when the toy drops on the floor. Other common early phrases are "what' sat?" "Mommy gone," and "bye-bye." When parents respond to these utterances, they help their children learn the words as well as how to interact in communication exchanges. By three years, your toddler's vocabulary will have exploded and she will routinely be combining three or more words into full sentences, will be talking constantly and beginning to comprehend concepts such as big and little. Infancy and toddlerhood is a critical and dramatic learning period for developing brain synapses for language acquisition.

Think about the following interaction between two parents and their one-year-old toddler.

The baby, Patrick, is sitting in a high chair with his father and says, "yayaya" and father copies him saying, "yayaya." Then Patrick says ba-ba and father waits and repeats ba-ba.

By three years, your toddler's vocabulary will have exploded and she will routinely be combining three or more words into full sentences.

The two go back and forth talking with ya-ya and ba-ba. Patrick says something else and his mother points to his bottle and says, "What is this?" and then she says, "This is milk."

This interaction shows how "parent-ese" works between a parent and child. The father is mirroring his son's language in a reciprocal dance of delight. Patrick is learning how his language affects his father's responses. His mother is showing and giving him the name for an object, in this case what he is drinking, "This is milk." These parents are helping their one-year-old begin to move from expressing his language in vowels to babbling to words and he is also learning to see how his language influences their social interactions.

TODDLER ALERT

Remember, learning to talk is hard work and needs practice. A pacifier (or dummy or binkie) will discourage your toddler from babbling and chatting with you, so if your toddler is still using one, ask her to take it out before you talk to each other.

Toddler-directed Descriptive Commenting

Research has indicated that parents around the world speak to babies in a kind of playful babbling way with lots of oohs, and ahs and use of simple sounds, vowels, and consonants. Studies have also shown that parents can help their babies and toddlers learn their language by modeling words for them and naming objects and actions in their world. This is called "descriptive commenting" and will contribute to your child's language development. You can start this language coaching by simply naming objects, colors, shapes, or positions of things you see in day-to-day life: on a walk, at the grocery store, or in your own kitchen. Talk about things your toddler shows interest in and point to the object as you name it. "Yes, the kitty is furry and brown. You can touch the kitty gently." "We need some apples today. There's a red apple going into the basket." Remember it is important to be child-directed in your communication with your toddler—that is, describe what your toddler is already doing or looking at. Don't be too directive with this commenting as this may interfere with her curiosity, exploration and sense of independence.

By one year babies understand many words, even though they may not produce much language. By three years most children understand conversational language and can participate in simple back and forth exchanges that have some real meaning. Just as with other developmental milestones, there is great variability in children's

> Talk about things your toddler shows interest in and point to the object as you name it.

normal language development. Some children are using words before the age of one and talking in simple sentences by two, and other two-year-olds still speak very few words, although they will understand language. Although you can check with your pediatrician if you are concerned, in most cases children's language development will progress at its own rate. Whether your child is an early or a late talker, using descriptive commenting will enhance her language skills. Since researchers think that acquiring language is essential to the development of thinking, your descriptive language will help your child's cognitive as well as language development.

TODDLER ALERT

If your toddler babbles infrequently, avoids looking at you, rarely uses gestures, such as pointing or imitating hand signals, such as waving "bye bye," or rarely copies sounds and seems unable to comprehend or say familiar words she has heard many times, seek consultation from a specialist in speech and language. This is a critical period for language development because the toddler's brain is so plastic and receptive to intervention. This means that if your child has real difficulties with language, the earlier these difficulties are detected and intervention is offered, the easier it will be for your child to make progress.

Limit Your Toddler's Exposure to Television and Media

Did you know that studies have shown that two-year-olds spend an average of twenty-seven hours a week watching TV, while parents spend only an average of five minutes of play time with their child each day? Research has shown that neither television nor computer programs (even if the programs are educational) enhance language development or academic achievement—your human interaction is essential to language learning! Before the age of two, it's recommended by the American Academy of Pediatrics that children do not watch any television at all. Once young children become addicted to television as a passive form of entertainment, they will be less likely to entertain themselves with books and physical activities. Remember, your toddler's healthy brain connections are not enhanced by watching television; rather, TV encourages short attention span, a passive brain, lower vocabulary, and often doesn't reflect your values. On the other hand, playing and reading with your toddler does enhance interactive dialogue and conversation, longer attention span, higher vocabulary and even problem solving skills. Don't be seduced by using TV as a baby sitter!

Even after the age of two, try to limit daily TV or DVDs to half an hour per day for two-year-olds and an hour for three- to five-year-olds. Be sure these are programs designed for this age group. Choose educational programs with no violence and characters who are positive role models. Also be aware of watching adult programs when your child is present. Children who witness violence on TV (even news programs) are more aggressive, more desensitized to violence, and more inclined to think the

Neither television nor computer programs enhance language development or academic achievement.

Human interaction is essential

world is a scary place than children who don't see this violence. Even if you think your toddler doesn't understand the news program, your toddler is learning from your emotional reactions to the programs. Take a look at your own TV viewing habits and adjust them for the healthy development of your children's brain nervous system.

When your children do watch TV, it is preferable to use DVDs or prerecorded television programs so that you can skip the commercials. Young children are vulnerable to advertising and the negative effects of advertising are evident even after children watch just a few commercials. Children do not understand the purpose of advertising and believe that what they watch is true. Thus, they are particularly susceptible to messages that junk food is desirable or that it's important to have a particular toy. Limit the number of channels that are available to reduce possible exposure to violence.

> Children who witness violence on TV (even news programs) are more aggressive, more desensitized to violence.

TODDLER ALERT

Also turn off your TV when no one is watching, for this background noise can be distracting to you and your child and can interfere with your toddler's ability to listen, pay attention and to talk to others. Remember muting your TV sound is not turning off the impact of TV, the visual picture will still distract you and your toddler's attention and you will be teaching your toddler how to be distracted. Instruct your babysitters, caretakers and grandparents about your rules regarding TV watching. Instead, show them some of the play activities from your play journal (page 71) that your toddler enjoys. Explain to them about the effects of TV watching on children's brain development.

Modeling and Prompting Words

One of the new behaviors a toddler engages in is pointing to things and looking at things that other people point to. Pointing is an important developmental landmark because it implies that your child understands the difference between herself and others. Toddlers can point to communicate something that they want. When this happens, you can help them learn words by modeling the words they could use.

Word modeling

In the next example a mother is playing outside with her three-year-old child, Kalani, using rocks, kitchen utensils, and a small pool of water—a no-cost but highly educational learning toy. Kalani is language delayed. In this interaction think about the strategies the mother is using to encourage her son's language expression and learning.

Kalani wants something (is pointing) and his mother asks, "Do you want the cup? Little cup?" She figures out he wants the strainer from his gestures and hands him the strainer. She models the words for him to use ("strainer please") to get what he wants. He imitates these words, "Strainer please," and his mother responds positively. Later Kalani wants the strainer again and he points to it urgently. His mother asks if he remembers the word and when he doesn't reply she prompts him by saying, "Strainer please." He repeats these words again and she hands him the strainer repeating the word strainer. Next he pours some water through the strainer and he discovers the water goes through the strainer. His mother says, "The water goes through the strainer." Then he puts his feet in the water and his mother tells him he is wet using sign language and also uses her words saying, " The water is making your feet wet." He indicates by pointing he wants more water – and mother models the words he can use, "More water please," as well as using sign language. He repeats, "Water–me."

This time Kalani picks up the strainer himself and his mother praises him for figuring out how to get the strainer. She hands him the water and he tries to pour it in the strainer but misses the strainer. Mother asks him if he is getting wet. He repeats, "More water" and mother says, "More water please" and he repeats, "More water please." She hands him more water and asks him if he wants to stay in the water or come out and he tells her "in." She hands him some more water. He is excited about pouring the water and asks again, "More water." Each time the mother repeats his words along with the sign language. Then she models saying thank you and is enthusiastic about his use of words.

We notice here that when Kalani points to something he wants, his mother names the object or what she thinks is his request and desire, and when he responds by imitating her words, she praises him. She is reinforcing his use of language through modeling, constant repetition, and praise. At times she also gently prompts him to see if she can get him to use his words to ask for what he wants and when he doesn't respond, she gives him the words and models what to say. She is not critical or demanding, is positive, gives encouraging smiles and follows his lead in the play. She fosters his sense of autonomy and independence by letting him make the decisions.

Toddlers can figure out what to do with objects by looking at what others do with them. In this case, Kalani's mother is helping him feel safe to explore the use of the strainer and water play while at the same time is reinforcing his use of language through modeling and repetition. She is encouraging his curiosity and discovery of how things work as well as his language.

Young children also learn about feelings by looking at how others feel. For example, if you smile, your toddler may walk forward to investigate, but if you have an expression of horror, your toddler will stop and turn to you for security. Have you noticed that if your child falls down and has a mild bump, she looks to you before reacting? If you respond in a reassuring voice: "Uh, oh. You fell down, but you can get up again," chances are that she'll get up and continue on her way. If you respond with alarm in your voice: "Oh, no! Are you okay?" she may cry and reach to you for comfort.

Toddlers can figure out what to do with and how to react to objects by looking at others' responses.

TODDLER ALERT

Talk in the language that you know best. It doesn't have to be English. For children in a bilingual environment, the number of words the child can speak will be split between the two languages she is learning. Find books in your own language or make up your own stories. Help your child feel proud of your language.

Preschool Readiness Coaching - ABCs and Colors

Once toddlers begin to learn the names for objects and actions, you can begin to expand their language repertoire by doing something we call "academic readiness coaching." This is when you describe things that will contribute to your child's preschool readiness or reading readiness. This can include naming numbers, letters, shapes, or colors. The objective is not to pressure your toddler to learn these things because it is still very early for these skills to develop. Instead just familiarize her with the concepts by naming them as part of your toddler-directed descriptive commenting. If your child repeatedly hears the vocabulary for these words and concepts at the same time that she is exploring and playing with the objects, she will begin to link the ideas with words long before she can produce the words herself. In the next example, a Chinese mother and her daughter are playing with an alphabet puzzle, which they clearly have done many times before. Think about the mother's academic readiness coaching methods.

Describing actions and naming objects

Jolie brings over an alphabet puzzle to work on with her mother. Jolie holds up the letter T – and her mother says T several times and then says, "You are holding the green letter T." Jolie repeats the name "T" several times. Then Jolie looks for where it goes on the puzzle and points to the empty space for "T." She looks at the place on the puzzle where the letter T goes and her mother says, "You are smart for remembering it

is a teddy bear." Jolie replies, "<u>Teddy</u> bear." The mother replies enthusiastically, "Yes you are right, it is a teddy bear!" Next the mother takes all the pieces out of the puzzle and Jolie begins to find the places for the letters. She finds the place for the letter "N" and her mother praises her by saying, "Good for finding the right place for the letter N." Whenever <u>Jolie</u> says the letter her mother repeats the name of the letter and praises her for getting the right letter. She also praises Jolie for working hard looking for the letters. The mother is very patient, giving Jolie time to explore and figure it out for herself. Again the mother praises her for working hard. At one point Jolie finds the spot for L and says, "L–lemon." Her mother repeats, "Good job, L is for lemon!" Jolie can't figure out where the next letter goes so eventually she tries a different letter and the mother doesn't interfere. The mother labels the colors of the letters in both Chinese and English.

Pay attention to the things that your own toddler is interested in and use your descriptive language to encourage her play. Avoid forcing your child to learn letters.

This rather remarkable toddler is able to recognize letters, colors, and positions of puzzle pieces, and to focus on the task for quite a long time. This is fairly unusual for children this age. In fact, children learn these skills at widely different rates and most toddlers won't have the persistence to do a complex letter puzzle. The important thing is that this mother is making this learning process fun and following her toddler's interests and readiness for learning. Pay attention to the things that your own toddler is interested in and use your descriptive language to encourage her play. Remember not to force your child to learn letters or do a puzzle, but if she is exploring puzzle pieces or looking at an alphabet book, you can label shapes, sizes, and colors. During the toddler years try to resist the temptation to compare your child with other children as there is a wide range of normal.

Avoid Too Much Question-Asking

Occasionally parents have a tendency to ask a string of questions while playing, "Why are you doing it that way?" "Is that the right color?" "What are you doing?" "How does it go on?" Through such questions, you usually intend to help your child learn, but all too often it has the reverse effect.

Asking too many questions when playing with your child can be intimidating to her and make her feel she has to perform for you – particularly if you know the answers to your questions! Too many questions from parents can cause children to refuse to speak and retreat into silence. So it is important to balance question asking with about ten times more descriptive comments and coaching statements than questions.

In the next example, a father and his four-year-old daughter are playing at a table with markers and paints.

As the girl paints, the father describes her actions, "You're going to paint the paint. Oh, you're painting orange on blue. Oh, that's orange on orange – very good! That's orange on purple – any other colors there? Let's see, orange on red, orange on yellow, really good."

This father describes the colors his daughter is using, rather than asking questions. This kind of describing is very reinforcing for children. It shows them that their parent is paying close attention to what they are doing. It communicates to them that their efforts are interesting and worthwhile. Furthermore, this kind of describing is a way of teaching concepts without having to ask a lot of questions. By hearing the names of the colors as she is playing, she will actually learn color names much faster than if her father had asked her to tell him the color names. Question asking, such as, "What color is that?" "Where does it go?" "How many animals are there?" tend to make children feel they have to perform for parents, particularly since the parents know the answers! Too

> Too many questions from parents can cause children to refuse to speak and retreat into silence.

many questions will cause your child to close up, refuse to answer and interfere with their curious exploration. On the other hand, descriptive commenting and academic readiness coaching will help your child to open up with a rich display of language and promote the discovery process.

In fact, question-asking, especially when you know the answer, is really a type of command or a test since it requires children to perform. Queries that ask your children to define what they are doing or why they are doing it a particular way are in a special category because they often occur before the child has even thought about the final product or had a chance to explore her ideas. Through the question, the parent puts the emphasis on the product rather than the process of play. Descriptive commenting, on the other hand, is a nonthreatening way of communicating with your children without demanding performance. Question-asking also breaks children's concentration and focus whereas commentary does just the opposite because it requires no answer.

On the other hand, the occasional question is not a problem and it can show that you are genuinely interested in your child's thoughts or ideas. For example, questions such as, "How can I help?" or "What should we do next?" are non-testing questions because the parent doesn't know the answer to the question in advance and is looking for some direction from the child. Think about the type of questions you ask your toddler. Are they test questions, or are they questions that help you know what help your child wants, or because you are genuinely interested in their idea?

> Descriptive commenting is a nonthreatening way of communicating with your children without demanding performance.

TODDLER ALERT

Parents should comprehend about half of child's speech at two years and about three quarters at three years. By four years, even people who don't know the child should understand most of what she says. Get an evaluation if after two years of age your child doesn't produce words spontaneously, or can't understand simple directions, or has an unusual tone of voice.

Promoting Reading Readiness – Modeling, Repetition, and Praise

Reading with your toddler is an important way of building her language and pre-reading readiness. Let your child pick out books on topics she is interested in. Find a quiet place to read and turn off the TV or telephone so there are no distractions. Start reading the book by taking the time to look at the cover. If your child seems interested, you can name the title, author, and illustrator. "This book is called *Goodnight*

Moon by Margaret Wise Brown. She wrote this story. Clement Hurd drew the pictures." As you read, keep your pace slow and follow your child's lead as you look at and talk about the pictures. You can have fun labeling or finding objects in the pictures as well as reading the real story words. You can extend the ideas in the pictures to your child's own experience. For example, if there is a picture of a dog or cat, talk with your toddler about a particular dog or cat that you know. "Yes, that's a cat. A cat just like Tigger from next door." Or talk about a time your child did something that is pictured in the book. "That swing looks like the one you played on yesterday at the playground. Do you remember that we went there with Zoey?" Don't put pressure

Praising

on your toddler to name the pictures, but if she copies your words, praise her and repeat the word. You can also extend her vocabulary by adding to her words. For example if your child points and says ball, you can repeat, "Yes, that is a ball. A big yellow ball." If there are sentences, run your finger under the words as you read them. If there are large letters on the page, you can name them and make the letter sound. You and your child can take turns sharing what you are seeing. Most of all, make looking at books fun and follow your child's attention span. Some toddlers may sit and look at several books at a time, while others may move on to another activity after one or two pages. Remember you don't need to read for too long. Toddlers get bored quickly and want to be active so shorter, more frequent

I make reading with my toddler fun

reading sessions often work best. The following is an example of another interaction between Kalani, who we talked about earlier, and his mother as they look at a book together.

Kalani, three years old, and his mother are reading a book together at the table. They are looking at a picture of a watermelon on the page. His mother comments that Kalani likes watermelon and that it is red. Then she points to the spider and names it verbally and with sign language. He repeats the word "Spider" and his mother praises him and expands on his language by telling him, "It is a purple spider." Next Kalani turns the page and says, "Bird." Kalani's mother repeats the word bird again in addition to sign language and she makes the sound of a bird. Next she observes that it is raining in the picture, and Kalani repeats the word "Raining." Then he sees a cow, and his mother asks him, "Is the cow is taking a bath?" On the last page of the book Kalani sees all the animals and makes the sound of a monkey. His mother names the word monkey. Then Kalani makes the sound of the bird and his mother names it. His mother notices a shape and he responds by naming all the shapes. She responds with excitement about his accomplishment.

Toddlers get bored quickly and want to be active so shorter, more frequent reading sessions often work best.

She gives him the opportunity to read on his own by letting him turn the pages and observing what he notices on each page.

Kalani has delayed language development and his mother is encouraging his language expression by naming the objects and showing him the sign language for the words. She gives him the opportunity to read on his own by letting him turn the pages and observing what he notices on each page. She models the words for him and is very encouraging when he imitates or mirrors her. With her fun approach incorporating the sounds of the animals, she is teaching him a love for reading. Undoubtedly he will want to repeat reading the same book many times, and as he does so he will begin to memorize it and feel confident about his ability to read the book and to identify the animals.

Read picture books

Reading Ideas:

- Have a box of books that your toddler can reach and select books from all on her own. Then when your toddler pulls a book from the box, describe what your child is looking at. Although this might not appear to be reading, it is building your toddler's vocabulary as well as the fine motor skills needed to hold the book and turn the pages.
- Order a subscription to a magazine for your toddler. There are many children's magazines with stories, poems, and pictures. You and your child will begin to look forward to the ritual of getting the magazine in the mail each month.
- Visit the library with your child and help her select a few books. Find out about story time at the library, or read books yourself with your child at the library. Children's librarians have great ideas for developmentally appropriate books, and most libraries have children's sections with comfortable chairs, puzzles or games for children. This is a free and valuable way to introduce your child to the world of literature!

Your toddler's attention for books will still be relatively short at this age and unpredictable. Sometimes your toddler may be content to sit and read for many minutes, other times she may start squirming or reaching for another book before the first page is done. This is developmentally normal. You can continue to encourage your toddler's reading by asking a question about the book or a picture, reading in a dramatic way, or continuing to read a few more pages even if your child has started to wander off. If your child looks at you, stops doing what she is doing, or comes back to the book you will know she is still interested in reading. However, if your toddler is really interested in something else, wait and read later when your child is not so driven to explore something else.

TODDLER ALERT

Take along books in cars and to doctor appointments or places where you might be waiting and you want to engage your child's attention.

Pre-writing Readiness

Coloring with toddlers is a lot of fun and is another opportunity to use descriptive and academic commenting. Did you know that it is also a way to encourage pre-writing skills? Give your toddler some big crayons on a large piece of paper or paper bag. Let your toddler scribble and draw on the page and talk about the colors and designs she is drawing. You can experiment with many different ways for your child to begin to learn the fine motor skills involved in writing: try drawing together in the sand with a stick, making designs with a finger in shaving cream on a tray, use bath crayons and draw on the side of the tub, or let your child decorate her tummy, or paint with brushes or finger paints. As your child creates her own art, use descriptive commenting to give words to her actions. For example, "Your blue line is going across the bottom of the page. Now your red line is on top of the page." Describe the kinds of lines your toddler is making. "That's a straight line going up the side of the bath tub. It looks like the letter I. Now there's a curvy line going across. That part is going around in circles like an O." If your child talks about what she is drawing or tells you a story about it, write it down on the bottom of the page and show delight in her story and the book she is making. These are all pre-reading and pre-writing skills.

As your child creates her own art, use descriptive commenting to give words to her actions.

Persistence Coaching

Persistence coaching is a method of talking to your toddler that will help her begin to learn to persist with difficult tasks and continue to try hard despite frustrations and difficulties. With this type of coaching, your toddler starts to recognize when she is concentrating, staying focused, being curious about discovering how something works and being calm or patient. Your toddler will also begin to learn that it is normal to struggle to learn something new but with patience, persistence, and your support, she can eventually accomplish the task and feel proud of it. This is an important life message.

As we discussed in chapter 1, children vary in their temperament and learning styles. Some toddlers are calm, quiet, slow to warm up, patient, focused, or attentive whereas others may be active, energetic, impulsive, inattentive, angry, or easily frustrated. Many children display more than one of these different traits at different times of day or in different situations. Despite these temperament variations, most toddlers will need parental support to be able to persist and stay patient with a task without getting overly frustrated. Some children will need more support than others. *Persistence coaching* is when the parent names the child's internal cognitive state when she is being patient, trying again, staying calm, concentrating, focusing or persisting and working hard with a difficult task. This type of coaching is beneficial for all children

Most toddlers will need parental support to be able to persist and stay patient with a task without getting overly frustrated.

Patience and persistence

but is particularly important for inattentive, impulsive, and hyperactive children. It helps them recognize times when they are focused, attentive and curious and what it feels like to be in that state. This coaching provides the brain scaffolding that a child needs to be able to stay calm and persistent for a few minutes longer than she would be able to do on her own.

The next example is a three-year-old girl, Soleil, who is doing an art drawing activity with her mother that involves cutting some sticky tape. Soleil is frustrated with her ability to cut and her mother uses persistence coaching (and emotion coaching) to give her enough support so that she continues to persist with the activity.

Soleil asks her mother for help cutting the sticky tape. Her mother says, "I will hold the tape while you cut. It is hard to cut." Soleil cuts the tape and her mother enthusiastically says, "You cut the tape yourself!" Soleil replies, "I cut it" and her mother asks, "Are you proud of yourself for cutting?" Soleil nods "Yes." Mother replies, "You seem very proud of your work, and you are working really hard. You keep trying." When Soleil cuts again, her mother says enthusiastically, "You did it" and then comments, "You seem happy with your work." As Soleil continues to work at cutting her mother comments, "You are working hard and being very patient with the cutting process. It seems to be getting easier and easier for you."

This mother's persistence coaching helps her daughter to stay involved and persist with a difficult task. She readily acknowledges that Soleil is attempting to do something that is very difficult, which adds to the sense of accomplishment for Soleil. This is a new kind of language for many parents. Statements such as, "you are working hard," "you are really focused," "that is frustrating and hard to do but you are staying patient with it," "you are really thinking what to do next," "you figured it out" or "you really concentrated and you solved the problem," are all examples of persistence coaching. This type of coaching can help your child modulate their feeling of frustration and stick with a difficult task without getting too dysregulated.

TODDLER ALERT

Your toddler is beginning the magic of discovering how things work and learning the language of how to talk about that. When you use coaching strategies which encourage your child's language, curiosity and persistence with her activity, you will see your child's face light up with delight. It is this magical connection that lies at the heart of your child's successful education.

Read and Talk in Your Own Language

Young children will readily learn more than one language, and this early exposure to a second language will help set the stage for eventual fluency in both languages.

If your native language is not English, make sure to speak to your child in your own language as much as possible, or as much as you want to. Since this is a critical period for language development, young children will readily learn more than one language, and this early exposure to a second language will help set the stage for eventual fluency in both languages. After age seven it becomes more difficult to learn a new language. Don't worry that your child won't learn English if you don't speak it at home. Your child will get plenty of exposure to English when she is in preschool. So do descriptive commenting and coaching in your own language, tell stories about your own family and culture, find books written in your own language, or try to make your own books. Don't laugh or tease your child if she has an accent or makes mistakes. Do not correct or make your child use a particular language. Also know that sometimes children who are exposed to more than one language are initially a little slower to use either language because they are sorting out the different sounds and meanings. Don't worry, these initial delays will go away eventually and your child will be able to distinguish between different syllables and use the two languages with ease after a while.

Language exposure

Keeping Developmental Expectations Appropriate —Laying the Brain Foundation for the Future

Developing concentration, persistence, and patience depends a lot on your child's particular temperament style and neurological, language, or brain development. These cognitive skills develop at different times and there is a wide range of normal development across children, just as there is for the motor skills of rolling over, sitting up, crawling or walking. Remember all toddlers have immature brain development and acquire skills in stages. Their ability to pay attention and follow directions, persist at something, or control their aggressive responses is at the very rudimentary physiological stages. At this stage your toddler has very little brain neurological self-control, self-regulation, and persistence. Your toddler will be able to start to link your words and prompts to her own self-control behavior if you are coaching her consistently, but likely will not be able to control her own reactions for quite a while. In other words, while you are near her actively saying, "You are really waiting for that toy. I see you want it, but you are waiting for your turn," you may be able to keep her from grabbing it out of another child's hand for a minute or two. As soon as you turn away, it is developmentally normal that she will forget your coaching and try to grab the toy. However, with repeated exposure to the concepts of being patient, calm, and persistent, she will begin to internalize these words. By the preschool years your child may be able to control somewhat more of her behavioral responses and attention span, but many children don't develop self-regulation skills, impulsivity, aggression, and ability to sustain their attention with a difficult task until five or six years. Certainly the development of language skills helps this self-regulation. So it is important for you to have realistic developmental expectations of your own child and of how much can be accomplished during the toddler years. Nonetheless, your academic and persistence coaching will be helping to lay a firm brain foundation to build on in later years.

> Remember all toddlers have immature brain development and acquire skills in stages.

Descriptive Commenting Feels Awkward at First

At first descriptive commenting, academic and persistence coaching may feel phony and artificial to you, and your child may comment on the new way that you are talking. Many children will notice that their parents are talking to them differently, particularly if they don't start using this kind of language until late toddlerhood or preschool years. Some children who have difficulty accepting change may ask their parents to, "Stop talking so weird." Don't be deterred by this negative response—it is to be expected! Whenever a parent behaves differently, children will initially resist the change in an effort to revert back to what is familiar and safe. However, with time, this form of communication will not only become the status quo in your interactions with your child but will be imitated by your children in their communication with siblings and friends. After a while you may find that your child looks

for your descriptive comments and may even start to ask you, "talk about what I'm doing." You will also find that after a while descriptive commenting will seem natural to you and you will do it without even thinking.

To Sum Up...

When you play with your toddler using a toddler-directed approach coupled with academic readiness and persistence coaching you are showing your child you are interested in what she is thinking and doing and that you enjoy being together. This strengthens both child and parent feelings of attachment in your relationship. In addition you are supporting your child's cognitive brain development for language and preschool readiness skills such as colors, shapes, letters, and vocabulary. You are also scaffolding your child's attention and beginning to help her learn how to stay focused and calm despite distractions and feelings of frustration. As you support all this learning and brain development, you are still attending to your toddler's need for autonomy and independent exploration. These are strategies that work not only with toddlers but with preschoolers too.

Points to Remember about
Promoting Toddlers' Language and Pre-school Readiness Skills

- Prompt your toddler to communicate by modeling the words for her to repeat.
- Praise your toddler's use of words.
- Chant and sing rhymes and teach your child body movements that go with the words.
- Use many more descriptive comments than questions.
- Describe your toddler's actions.
- Praise and give positive feedback to your toddler (that's right!)
- Describe your toddler's body parts and feelings
- Listen to your toddler and imitate, or mirror, your toddler's words
- Notice what your toddler is interested in and talk about it
- Describe the objects, shapes, numbers, letters and colors of toys your toddler plays with.
- Describe your own actions to your toddler (e.g, "I'm going to the kitchen now).
- Tell your toddler you love him or her and share feelings of joy.
- Notice when your toddler is working hard, concentrating, being calm, staying patient with a frustrating activity, trying again, and name or describe this persistence.
- Read to your toddler often.
- Give your child opportunities to color and describe his actions.
- Talk about positions of objects (e.g., inside, under, beside, next to).

- Talk about simple every day stories and events.
- Use puppets to make up stories with your toddler.
- Use make believe games such as toy telephones or hand puppets to encourage talking.
- Try to really understand what your toddler is saying.
- Use new words to expand her vocabulary even if you know she won't understand at first.

I use new words with my child

Points to Remember about
Reading with Your Toddler

- Read at a quiet time when you are relaxed and comfortable–with TV and music turned off (this prevents over stimulation).
- Allow your child to select the book from her favorites and turn the pages at will.
- Hold your toddler in a comfortable position on your lap when reading; or if she is squiggly allow her to read lying down or standing up.
- Read for a few minutes each day when your toddler seems calm and alert. (Reading at bedtime is a great routine to have established because it helps your toddler calm down.)
- If you have other children, read to them as well.
- Use "parent-ese" language when reading, because this is preferred by toddlers over regular communication. Parent-ese sounds like this:

    -singsong, higher pitched, slower voice
    -clear articulation (not baby talk)
    -pauses longer after speaking to wait for response
    -words repeated often
    -uses an exaggerated facial expression (big smiles) when responding
    -expressive voice using sound effects (for animals, cars, actions)

I repeat words often

- Point to pictures in the book and talk about them or make up stories.
- Re-read books your toddler likes many times.
- Chant and sing rhymes.

- Use hand movements with words.
- Praise and give positive feedback (that's right!).
- Slide your finger under the words or letters on the page and show left to right movement.
- Encourage your toddler to turn the pages.
- Read the names of the author and illustrator to your toddler as you begin reading.
- Go to the library together for story time or just to browse. Let your child pick several books to take home.
- Read books that reflect your toddler's experience such as having a bath, putting on boots for the rain; books that use phrases such as good-bye, thank you; books that ask questions; books with rhymes and songs with hand movements.
- For 12-18-month-old toddlers–read books that encourage your toddler to chime in and repeat words; books that label objects and parts of the body; books that illustrate action words such as walking or running; and books with flaps or noises.
- For 18-24 month old toddlers–read books about your toddler's interests (boats, trucks); books that include hand movements; books with numbers, colors, shapes; books with stories that show feelings.

Prevent over stimulation

Remember, toddlers have a wide range in attention span that will vary daily. Don't worry if your toddler seems restless and gets off your lap. Keep reading. If she seems more interested in another activity, wait and try to read again later.

Most toddlers will want to have the same book read over and over again. This is important to them because it provides security and allows them to memorize the book so they get a feeling of mastery over the book. Then they may even read the book back to you! It is an important pre-reading skill.

I read the same book over and over

Points to Remember about
Building Blocks for Reading with CARE

Comment, use descriptive commenting to describe pictures.
- Take turns interacting, and let your child be the storyteller by encouraging him/her to talk about the pictures.

Ask open-ended questions.
- "What do you see on this page?" (observing and reporting)
- "What's happening here?" (storytelling, encouraging being curious)
- "What is that a picture of?" (promoting academic skills)
- "How is she feeling now?" (exploring feelings)
- "What is going to happen next?" (predicting)

Respond with praise and encouragement to your child's thinking and responses.
- "That's right!"
- "You are really thinking about that."
- "Wow, you know a lot about that."

I read with CARE to my child

Expand on what your child says.
- "Yes, I think he's feeling excited, too, and he might be a little scared as well."
- "Yes, it is a horse; it's also called a mare."
- Yes, that boy is going to the park. Do you remember going to the park?"

I use academic coaching

Points to Remember about
Coaching Toddlers' Language & Pre-School Readiness Skills

"Descriptive commenting" in the form of academic coaching and persistence coaching is a powerful way to strengthen your children's language skills. The following is a list of actions, behaviors and objects that can be commented upon when playing with your child. Use this checklist to practice and reflect on your coaching skills.

ACADEMIC COACHING: OBJECTS, ACTIONS, SHAPES, POSITIONS	EXAMPLES
☑ colors, letters	"You have the red car and the yellow truck."
☑ number counting	"There are one, two, three dinosaurs in a row."
☑ shapes	"Now the square Lego is stuck to the round Lego."
☑ names of objects	"That train is longer than the track."
☑ sizes (long, short, tall, smaller than, bigger than, etc.)	"You are putting the tiny bolt in the right circle."
☐ positions (up, down, beside, next to, on top, behind, etc.)	"The blue block is next to the yellow square, and the purple triangle is on top of the long red rectangle."

Persistence Coaching: Cognitions and State of Mind

Examples

- ❑ working hard
- ❑ concentrating, focusing

"You are working so hard on that puzzle and thinking about where that piece will go."

- ❑ staying calm, patient
- ❑ trying again

"You are so patient and just keep trying all different ways to make that piece fit together."

- ❑ problem solving
- ❑ thinking skills

"You are staying calm and trying again."

- ❑ reading
- ❑ going to do it

"You are thinking hard about how to solve the problem and coming up with a great solution to make a ship."

Coaching Preschool Readiness Behaviors

Examples

- ☑ following parents' directions
- ❑ listening to parents

"You followed directions exactly like I asked you. You really listened."

- ☑ independence
- ☑ exploring and trying out ideas

"You have figured that out all by yourself."

Social & Emotional
Developmental Milestones
19–24 MONTHS

- Enjoys helping around the house (19 months)
- Understands most of what you say–about 200 words (19–20 months)
- Still loves rhymes and songs repeated (all months)
- Recognizes when something is wrong (19–20 months)
- Captivated by visual illustrations in books (20 months)
- Points to picture when you name it (20 months)
- Can say 50-100 or more words–learns at a rate of 10 or more per day! (20–24 months)
- Imitates expressions (even swear words!)
- Imitates what you do (clean table, wash dishes) (20 months)
- Does pretend play such as feed baby doll (20 months)
- Can identify and name several body parts (20 months)
- Learns how to form a question–"why" (21–22 months)

Imitates expressions

- Starts using action words (e.g., more, eat) *yes*
- Name simple picture in book (22 months) *yes*
- Sings simple tunes (23–24 months) *yes*
- Begins to be interested in playing with other children (24 months) *yes*
- Half of speech can be understood (24 months) *yes*
- Can make 2–3 word phrases ("me go") (24 months) *yes*

Physical Developmental Milestones
19–24 MONTHS

Solves simple puzzles

- Uses fork and spoon (19 months) needs work
- Can take off clothes (20 months) yes
- Can walk up but not down stairs (20–21 months) yes both
- Stacks 6 blocks (21–22 months) yes
- Does simple puzzles (22–23 months) NO
- Puts on loose clothing (23–24 months) yes

CHECKLIST FOR REFLECTING ON MY TODDLER'S PLAY

Complete this checklist first to reflect on your toddler's play and the nature of your child's temperament. When you observe your child's play, how often does he or she...

	ALMOST ALWAYS	SOMETIMES	NEVER
1. Seem joyful?	☑	☐	☐
2. Show curiosity?	☑	☐	☐
3. Try to speak (with babbles or conventional words)?	☐	☐	☑
4. Try out new ideas?	☑	☐	☐
5. Get frustrated easily?	☐	☑	☐
6. Seem passive?	☐	☑	☐
7. Display independence rather than dependence?	☐	☑	☐
8. Have short attention span and act impulsively?	☑	☐	☐
9. Show self-confidence?	☑	☐	☐
10. Rarely interact or seem interested in other children?	☐	☑	☐

	ALMOST ALWAYS	SOMETIMES	NEVER
11. Initiate interactions with peers?	❑	☑	❑
12. Respond to your questions or prompts by pointing or attempting words?	❑	☑	❑
13. Imitate what you are doing?	❑	☑	❑
14. Copy what you are saying?	☑	❑	❑

Parents' Viewpoint

CHECKLIST FOR REFLECTING ON MY PARENT-TODDLER PLAY INTERACTIONS

After completing your toddler's play interactions, use this checklist to self-reflect on your play interactions with your toddler. Use this self-reflection to make some goals for yourself during your play times.

A. When playing with my child, how often do I encourage my child to:

	ALMOST ALWAYS	SOMETIMES	NEVER
1. Explore?	☑	☐	☐
2. Make her own choices?	☑	☐	☐
3. Be creative and curious?	☑	☐	☐
4. Express feelings and ideas?	☐	☑	☐
5. Engage in pretend or make-believe play?	☑	☐	☐
6. Participate in both boys' and girls' play activities?	☐	☐	☐

B. When playing with my child, how often do I:

	ALMOST ALWAYS	SOMETIMES	NEVER
1. Direct or structure my child's activity?	☐	☑	☐
2. Follow my child's rules for the activity?	☑	☐	☐
3. Criticize and correct my child's mistakes?	☐	☐	☑

B. *(continued)* **When playing with my child, how often do I:**

	ALMOST ALWAYS	SOMETIMES	NEVER
4. Observe and give attention to what my child is interested in?	☑	☐	☐
5. Allow participation only in sex-appropriate activities?	☐	☐	☑
6. Feel uncomfortable with my child's expression of fear or helplessness?	☐	☐	☑
7. Let my child win at a game?	☐	☑	☐
8. Become engrossed in my own play, and ignore my child's play?	☐	☐	☑
9. Ask a lot of questions?	☐	☐	☑
10. Describe my child's feelings?	☑	☐	☐
11. Give my child a chance to help me?	☐	☑	☐
12. Model or engage in pretend play?	☐	☑	☐
13. Express my feelings of joy while playing with my child?	☐	☑	☐
14. Use persistence coaching (rather than focus on the ultimate product?)	☐	☑	☐
15. Use academic coaching?	☐	☑	☐

C. What interferes with my ability to play with my child?

My goals for myself when playing with my toddler are (write below):

Parents' Viewpoint
Thoughts About Play

Write down the benefits of child-directed play with your child and your difficulties in doing it. See if you can find any solutions to your barriers to playing with your child.

BENEFITS OF MY PLAYING AND COACHING MY CHILD	DIFFICULTIES IN DOING THIS

WAYS I WILL OVERCOME THESE BARRIERS

GOAL:

I will commit to playing with my child _____ times this week for _____ minutes.

Parent's Viewpoint
My Academic and Persistence Coaching Journal

Write your favorite coaching statements.

Toddler's Viewpoint
THINGS I CAN DO (19–24 months)

Activity	Date	Observations/Comments
Ask me to help, I love it		
I understand most of what you say		
I love songs and rhyming		
I know when you are upset		
I love to look at pictures in a book		
If you point to a picture I can name it		

Toddler's Viewpoint
THINGS I CAN DO (19–24 months)

Activity	Date	Observations/Comments
I am good at imitating expressions		
I like to do pretend play		
My fantasy play doesn't involve others		
I know some parts of my body		
I play with my feet		
I am beginning to form a question		

Toddler's Viewpoint
THINGS I CAN DO (19–24 months)

Activity	Date	Observations/Comments
I can sing a simple tune		
I can make 2-3 word phrases		
I can use a fork now		
I can take off my clothes		
I can walk up but not down stairs		
I can try a simple puzzle		

Toddler's Viewpoint
THINGS I CAN DO (19–24 months)

Activity	Date	Observations/Comments
I can try to dress myself		
I am very active		
I can throw a ball		
I can jump		
I love to read with you		

MY TODDLER'S PICTURE
(19–24 months)

CHAPTER 3

Coaching Toddlers' Social and Emotional Competence

Introduction

In chapter two we learned about two aspects of the coaching level of the parenting pyramid discussed earlier, in particular how academic and persistence coaching helps strengthen your toddler's language acquisition and helps teach the beginning preschool readiness concepts and skills. This chapter describes two more types of parental coaching: social coaching and emotion coaching.

You will learn how to use these coaching strategies with your toddler in order to begin his learning about initiation of friendship skills as well as to help him learn how to recognize and label his own feelings and the feelings of others. This coaching will also contribute to your toddler's ability to achieve key developmental milestones of communication, enhanced sense of self, and secure attachment to parents and other family members.

Social Coaching

Children under the age of two or three are egocentric and have very few prosocial skills.

Did you know that social skills need to be modeled, repeated, supported and encouraged, a process similar to what is needed for children's language acquisition or for development of physical skills? Remember how you supported and safely scaffolded your baby as he moved from the stages of head control, to sitting, to pulling to stand and to eventual walking? Your baby didn't learn walking skills instantly, he did this through a process of stages, or literally steps. Your interactions and level of support were adjusted with your understanding of what your baby was physically capable of handling. A parallel step by step process also occurs for children as they learn to become socially and emotionally mature. Children under the age of two or three are egocentric and have very few prosocial skills, especially with their peers. Toddlers rarely share, wait, or take turns! This is the age of "mine–mine–mine," and "I want what I want when I want it!" and curious exploration. Moreover, when toddlers play with other peers they usually engage in what is called "parallel play." That is children are playing next to each other but are not initiating interactions with each other and they are probably unaware of what each other is doing because they are so absorbed in their own discoveries. This may be true even for many preschool children. While this is normal developmental play for this age, you can still begin social teaching with your toddler. For social skills such as sharing, asking, being polite, listening, waiting,

Mine, mine, mine

and taking turns are determined both by your child's developmental abilities and temperament as well as by the coaching your child receives from interactions with you. You can begin to encourage your children to learn appropriate social skills by engaging in what we call "social coaching" which includes modeling, prompting, practicing, and praising specific social skills.

You can begin to encourage your children to learn appropriate social skills by engaging in what we call "social coaching."

Modeling Social Skills and Empathy
During Parent-Toddler One-on-One Play

The first aspect of social coaching involves parents modeling appropriate social skills themselves during parent-child play interactions. Remember that babies learn by imitating or modeling what you do and say and even mirror the feelings shown on your face! Toddlers learn in the same way. When you play, try to be respectful of their ideas, share your positive feelings, smile, offer friendly suggestions, compliment them, help with a difficult activity, comply with

Modeling social behaviors & language

their requests, and cooperate. Your toddler will be learning all these important social and relationship skills just by watching you demonstrate them in your play times with them. These are all behaviors that are hard for a toddler to learn in a play interaction with a same age peer because the other toddler doesn't have the developmental ability to engage in or model these positive interactive behaviors himself. When a parent or another adult plays with a child, this modeling can take place. Think about what the parent is modeling in the following example of a mother and her 18–month-old daughter who are each playing with play dough, cookie cutters, a rolling pin, and other wooden kitchen utensils on a kitchen table.

The mother says to her daughter, <u>Kyla</u>, who has cut out a play dough butterfly with her cookie cutter, "You made a pretty butterfly," and Kyla replies, " Make monster." Her mother replies with eagerness, "That's a good idea, I would like to see your monster." Next she notices that Kyla needs more play dough and she offers, "I can see you need more play dough for your monster, I will be your friend and share my play dough with you. Would you like my green play dough?" Kyla takes the play dough from her mother's outreached hand and the mother says, "Thank you" and Kyla replies, "Tank you." Mother replies, "That was very polite."

In this example the mother is both modeling and labeling the social skills of praise, agreement to another's idea, sharing, offering to help, and polite behavior. Notice that the mother described her own social behavior when she said, "I will be your friend and share my play dough with you" so that her daughter, Kyla, can learn what it means to share and that this behavior is something friends do with each other. The mother also shares with her toddler her own understanding of her toddler's mind when she said, "I can see you need more play dough for your monster." Thus she is modeling thinking about someone else's point of view or desires, a concept that is called developing "theory of mind." First, this mother models an awareness of her daughter's needs and then labels her need. Later the mother can extend this idea to her daughter's awareness of her friends' needs.

Remember that toddlers learn by imitating or modeling what you do and say.

Empathic modeling

Prompting and Encouraging Social Skills and Empathy During Parent-Toddler One-on-One Play

Modeling is when you model or demonstrate the social behaviors that you would like to see your child exhibit, such as when Kyla's mother modeled saying, "thank you" which showed Kyla what the appropriate language response was in that interaction. Prompting, on the other hand, is when you subtly prompt your child to use a particular social behavior. For example, you can "prompt" a child's social behavior during play by asking for help with your toy, offering an idea, or asking for a turn with something your child is using. If your child responds to your prompt by accepting your request for help, using your idea, or giving you a turn, then you coach their friendly response by clearly and positively describing their social skill. For example, first you prompt, "Could I have a turn with the shovel?" Your child says yes and gives you the shovel. You reply, "That was so friendly. I wanted the shovel and you shared it with me." This prompt and parental response is encouraging the toddler to understand someone else's perspective—a beginning step towards empathy or a theory of mind. However, if your child does not agree to share or help when you use a prompt, just ignore this response and model waiting and respect by saying, "I can see you are not ready to share yet, and I can wait for a turn. I'll play with the bucket while I wait." Again, this response indicates the parent is modeling her understanding of her toddler's perspective.

> You can "prompt" a child's social behavior during play by asking for help with your toy.

Remember a toddler is in the "mine" stage of development. One- to three-year-olds are absorbed with their own learning, will be possessive, are searching for independence, and aren't developmentally ready to share or to understand another's perspective. This is normal. Don't force your toddler to share, for this will defeat your purpose. However, you can begin to teach your toddler how to share or help others by modeling these behaviors yourself, prompting it occasionally, naming it and praising it whenever it does occur. It will often be easier for your toddler to share with you or another adult than it will be to share with a peer, so parent-child sharing is a good place to start. See if you can identify the "modeling" and "prompts" by Kyla's mother as they continue to play.

Social behavior prompts

Kyla asks her mother to make a worm for her out of play dough and her mother agrees and starts making it. Kyla says, "Thank you" spontaneously and her mother replies with a smile, "You are welcome." Then she asks Kyla, "Can I have some more of your blue play dough? I don't have enough to make a big worm." Kyla responds by handing her some more blue play dough and her mother replies, "Thank you for sharing with me. That was friendly." A few minutes later, the mother says, "It is getting so long and big I think I need some help." Kyla starts working with her on the worm and her mother replies, "Wow, thank you Kyla you are such a helper, we are a team and are making this together, this is fun."

It is important to model and prompt social behaviors and enthusiastically describe them through coaching language whenever they occur.

TODDLER ALERT

Don't force your toddler to share or be upset if he ignores your prompts to share. This is normal and means that your child is absorbed in his own discoveries. Instead, model the social behavior yourself and try to have 10 times more descriptive comments or coaching statements than prompts. Keep your expectations developmentally appropriate. Remember toddlers are a "work in progress."

Social Coaching: For parent-child play (level 1)

The following list provides some examples of the script for one-on-one parent social coaching. You can think of this as learning a new language to speak with your children. You might want to write some of these statements down to have handy to practice while you are playing with your child. It may feel awkward at first but like learning any language with practice it gets easier.

SOCIAL/FRIENDSHIP SKILLS   EXAMPLES

PARENT MODELS:

• **Sharing**	"I'm going to be your friend and share my car with you."
• **Offering to Help**	"If you want, I can help you with that by holding the bottom while you put another on top."
• **Waiting**	"I can use my waiting muscles and wait until you're finished using that."
• **Suggesting**	"Could we build something together?"
• **Complimenting**	"You are so clever in figuring out how to put that together."
• **Behavior-to-Feelings**	"You shared with me. You knew I wanted to play with that too. That is so friendly and makes me feel happy."
	"You helped me figure out how to do that. I feel proud that you could show me that."

PARENT PROMPTS:

• **Self-Talk**	"Hmm, I really wish I could find another piece to fit here."
	"Hmm, I'm not sure I know how to put this together."

SOCIAL/FRIENDSHIP SKILLS	EXAMPLES
Asking for help	"Can you help me find another round piece?"
	"Can you share one of your cars with me?"
	"This is hard, I might need some help."

PARENT RESPONSE:

• **Praise child when s/he shares or helps you**

"That was so helpful and friendly to share with me."

• **Ignore or model acceptance when child does NOT share or help**

Continue to use descriptive commenting.

"I can keep trying to find that round piece." (model persistence)

"I can wait until you're finished playing with the cars." (model waiting)

"I know it is hard to give up that car, so I will wait to have a turn later."

PUPPET OR ACTION-FIGURE MODELS:

• **Entering Play**

"Can I play with you?"

"That looks like fun. Can I do that with you?"

• **Being Socially Friendly**   "I'm being friendly. I'd like to play with you."

• **Ignoring Aggression**   "I want to play with a friendly person. I think I will find somebody else to play with."

Peer Social Coaching

One-on-one parent-child social coaching is immensely valuable for parents both for modeling and promoting social skills in their children but also for strengthening the special parent-child bond and intimacy in their relationship. Peer social coaching is somewhat different than parent-child coaching because now you are facilitating the social interactions and relationships between several children rather than just with you. For example, you comment on times when children initiate interactions with each other, notice what a peer is doing or needs help with, share with others, wait and take turns, and use their words to ask before grabbing a toy away from a peer. This social coaching will strengthen your child's ability to learn social skills and to develop first friendships. However, it is important to recognize that most toddlers are not developmentally ready to share, or wait and take turns. And some are more impulsive, inattentive and active than others so these social skills will be particularly difficult. Toddlers and many preschoolers are still in the age of exploration and discovering their sense of self and autonomy. It is not until late preschool or early school age years that your one-on-one and peer social coaching efforts will truly show some payoff. Remember, coaching, describing, and modeling social behaviors with your toddler during this time is providing the necessary brain scaffolding and foundation needed for your child's later social and emotional learning and behavior. Like the baby learning to walk, toddlers need to be supported and to be developmentally ready before they can use these social skills on their own.

In the next example, Kyla is seated next to her friend Jolie, another 18-month-old. They are each playing with play dough and seem completely unaware of each other's

Facilitate social interactions

This social coaching will strengthen your child's ability to learn social skills and to develop first friendships.

presence. This is normal parallel play for their age. See if you can pick out the prompts and peer coaching skills the same mother uses to try to facilitate some interactions and her child's use of social skills.

The mother notices Kyla wants a different color play dough and says to her, "I can see you want a different color, you can ask Jolie for the green play dough by saying, 'Can I use this please?'" Kyla keeps playing with her blue play dough without responding. Mother repeats the words she can use two more times saying, "Kyla you can say, 'can I use this?'" Kyla seems to ignore her prompt and Jolie continues making cookies from her green play dough and does not share. Kyla finally says, "Please use" and Jolie continues playing, seemingly unaware of the request. Kyla's mother says, "Kyla that is good asking and using your words, I think Jolie will let you have it when she is done with it. Can you wait your turn? Let's make that blue monster while we are waiting. You are doing very good waiting." Kyla gives her mother a spoon and her mother thanks her and praises her for nice sharing, and asks her if she is going to make a scary monster. Then she describes Jolie's work making cookies by saying, "Jolie, you are working hard on cooking. That green heart cookie looks yummy." Jolie responds by handing some of her green play dough to Kyla who seems not to notice. Mother responds, "Thank you Jolie. That is very friendly sharing" and she points out to Kyla, "Your friend Jolie is sharing her green play dough with you. You can say 'Thank you.'" Kyla says, "Thank you" and her mother replies, "You're welcome" and Jolie repeats this. Mother prompts Kyla, "Can you share some of your blue play dough with your friend, Jolie?"

Without this mother's social coaching, these two children would have played independently for awhile without noticing each other, probably until one of them grabbed what they wanted from the other and created some crying or unhappiness. This coaching was necessary for them to have this opportunity to learn what words to use to ask for

what they want, to be able to wait, and even to be aware of each other's requests, needs or helping behaviors. They are at the beginning stages of learning what it means to be friendly, to share with each other and to recognize another person's needs.

TODDLER ALERT
Don't say to your child, "Use your words" as toddlers likely don't know what words to use. Instead model or gently suggest to them the words they can use. If they copy your words, praise them and if they ignore you, let it go.

Social Coaching: For play with peers (level 2)

The following list provides some examples of the script for parent social coaching with more than one child. Remember that without your coaching, toddlers are unlikely to initiate much interactive play and will likely have conflicts over things that each other wants. With this type of social coaching, you will prompt the children to notice each other's moods and activities and will help support their social interactions. You can still use all the one-on-one coaching tips from the parent-child coaching, using yourself as another prosocial model in the interactions.

SOCIAL/FRIENDSHIP SKILLS	EXAMPLES
PARENT COACHES:	
• **Asking for What They Want**	"You can ask your friend for what you want by saying, 'Please can I have the crayon?'"
• **Asking for Help**	"You can ask your friend for help by saying 'Can you help me?'"
• **Asking a Friend to Wait**	"You can tell your friend you are not ready to share yet."
	If your child responds to your prompt by using his or her words to repeat what you said, praise this polite asking or friendly helping.

I promote social skills

SOCIAL/FRIENDSHIP SKILLS	EXAMPLES
PARENT PROMPTING:	
• **Noticing Other Child**	"Wow, look what a big tower your friend is building."
	"You are both using green markers."
• **Initiate Interaction With Other Child**	"Your friend is looking for small green pieces. Can you find some for him?"
	"Your friend has no cars and you have 8 cars. He looks unhappy. Can you share one of your cars with your friend?"
• **To Give Child a Compliment**	"Wow! You can tell your friend his tower is cool."
	If you child does repeat this, you can praise him or her for a friendly compliment.
	If your child does not respond, continue descriptive commenting.
PARENT PRAISING:	
• **Behavior-to-Feelings**	"You shared with your friend, that is so friendly and makes her feel happy."
	"You helped your friend figure out how to do that, she looks very pleased with your help."
	"Good waiting your turn with the green play dough."

SOCIAL/FRIENDSHIP SKILLS	EXAMPLES
• **Playing Together**	"Your friend is enjoying playing with these Legos with you. You look like you are having fun with your friend. You are both very friendly."

PUPPET OR ACTION-FIGURE MODELS:

• **Sharing or Helping**	"Wow! Do you see the tower that Nancy is building?"
	"Can either of you help me find a red block to make this truck?"
	"Could I help you build that house?" "Do you think we could ask Freddy if he'll share his train?"

Coach, Prompt, Praise

Social Skills Training with Siblings of Different Ages and Developmental Stages

Sibling coaching

One-on-one play times between parents and children are to be treasured and it is ideal to find ways to do at least some individual play time daily with each of your children. However, the practicalities of everyday life mean that there are many times when a parent will need to know how to facilitate play between siblings. All of the above ideas for coaching level 2 peer play will be useful when coaching siblings of different ages. However, you will also need to take into account that there are additional challenges to accommodate the differing developmental levels of older and younger siblings. Toddlers cognitively are not able to understand rules in games, nor do they developmentally have the ability to wait and take turns. This can make it especially difficult for them to play games with older school-age children who are obsessed by the rules. Without parent support, play between early school age children and toddlers may lead to bullying of younger children. It is important that toddlers not be criticized by parents or older siblings for this inability to understand the rules of a game because it is part of normal development for their age and something they can't help. It is also important to help protect an older child's games and possessions from the destructiveness of a toddler who can easily ruin a complicated Lego model or art project that the older sibling spent hours building. Thus, when coaching siblings, parents need to be sensitive to protecting the younger child from the unrealistic expectations of the older child, while at the same time protecting the older child from the impatience and tantrums of the younger child. With patience, parents can coach siblings in such a way that older children learn the skills of being empathic and forgiving of younger children. If you enlist

If you enlist your older children in the process, they can actually be great models of positive social skills.

your older children in the process, they can actually be great models of positive social skills for their younger siblings. This sibling modeling is particularly powerful because young children often idolize their older siblings. See if you can identify the strategies the father in the next scenario is using to promote social skills between his 18-month old daughter, preschool cousin, and his eight-year-old son who are all playing with bicycles on the sidewalk.

Father suggests his toddler use her words to ask her four-year-old cousin to use his tricycle. Father models the words for her to use by saying, "Tell him, 'please can I ride it?'" When her cousin shares his bike, the father prompts his daughter to say, 'Thank you' and shows appreciation for the cousin's sharing with her. Next the father encourages his eight-year-old son, Matias, to share his two-wheel bike with his cousin, who has given up his tricycle to the toddler. The father praises Matias for sharing by saying, " Thank you for thinking of your cous-in's feeling. That was very kind. Can you help your sister on the tricycle?" Father then helps the four-year-old to learn how to ride the two-wheeler while Matias gives his little sister a lot of encouragement for trying to ride by herself and helps her put her feet on the pedals. Father thanks Matias for his help, "Wow you have taught your sister how to use a tricycle. You are a great big brother, I'm proud of how you helped me with the children, everyone had a good time."

The toddler is learning about using her words to ask for what she wants.

In this interaction all the children are learning social skills as a result of this father's social coaching. The toddler is learning about using her words to ask for what she wants and to be polite when she gets what she wants. She is learning from the modeling and prompting by her father as well as her older brother's encouragement and

helping behaviors. The eight-year-old is also learning to be patient and caring with his younger sister. He sees how his father treats the younger children and then imitates this behavior with his sister. He receives praise from his father and then passes this praise on to his sister. Without this father's coaching, none of this learning would have likely happened. Instead each of the older children would have kept riding their own bikes and the toddler would have seemed to be in their way.

TODDLER ALERT
Don't let older siblings criticize or bully toddlers for not understanding games. Help them have realistic expectations, be patient and empathic to a toddler's world view. At the same time protect and respect the older sibling's need for privacy and freedom to play more complicated games without toddler interference.

Here is another example of a parent coaching her two children. Lia, a two-year-old, and four-year-old Daniel are playing in the living room with pots and pans, cupcake tins, some fish crackers and wooden kitchen spoons.

Daniel asks his sister <u>Lia</u> to put the crackers in the bowl and not in the cupcake tin. Mother repeats Daniel's request to Lia and models what to do by putting her own crackers in the bowl. Then Lia copies her putting her crackers in the bowl as well. <u>Mother praises and hugs Lia for listening and following her brother's directions.</u> Mother then prompts Daniel, "Daniel did you see that Lia did what you asked her to do?" Daniel stirs the crackers in the bowl with a spoon and suggests they now need some liquid. Mother hands him a pan of pretend warm milk (modeling cooperation). Lia asks for more milk too and *mother lets Daniel know that Lia wants more milk. Daniel says, "I need more crackers." Lia says, "mine" and points to her crackers. Mother confirms that they are Lia's crackers. Mother asks Lia, "Do you want to share any of the crackers with Daniel?" She says, "No—mine." Mother asks Daniel for some ideas for what they will do and then Daniel notices Lia has put some of her crackers in his bowl. He says, "Look she put some of her crackers in my bowl." (He is now noticing his sister's social skill.) Mother replies, "Lia you listened to Daniel and you are both playing together to build the same cake." (Mother reinforces Lia's behavior and Daniel's words.) Then Mother prompts Daniel by saying, "You can ask Lia to put more crackers in your bowl." He asks her politely and Mother praises his polite asking.*

This mother does a combination of prompting behaviors, descriptive commenting of social behaviors to get her children to notice each other, modeling of social skills, and praising her children's efforts. This back and forth prompting and coaching is teaching both children appropriate social interactions and will lead to positive sibling relationships.

Coaching of sibling interactions is probably one of the most exhausting tasks for parents. It often involves a juggling act, with the parent trying to alternate his or her praise, attention, and encouragement between the two (or more children) who are each wanting their parents' undivided attention. It involves meeting the developmental needs of more than one age group and being able to see the interaction from the different points of view of each child. In the long run, this sibling coaching will pay off and will result in siblings who have closer relationships, who are more socially skilled, and who are able to be flexible with children of all ages.

Coaching of sibling interactions is probably one of the most exhausting but worthwile tasks for parents.

Emotion Coaching Leads to More Behavioral Self-Regulation

Another kind of coaching that is helpful for young children is called "emotion coaching." This communication approach helps children begin to develop feelings literacy, that is, a vocabulary for expressing their emotions to you and others.

You start this coaching by naming your toddler's emotions whenever you see he is experiencing an emotion such as being happy, content, confident, surprised, curious, proud, brave, frustrated, sad, lonely, disappointed, tense, or angry. By labeling the feeling when you observe it in your child's behavioral reactions or facial expressions, he will learn the word for that feeling. Once children have developed an emotion vocabulary, they can then recognize their feeling and share their feelings with others. This results in their ability to more easily regulate their emotional and behavioral responses. Did you know that most preschoolers only know 2.5 words for feelings—mad and sad and sometimes happy? Even then, they often don't know the difference between mad and sad. The goal is to help children to have a bigger vocabulary to express their feelings, hopefully to recognize more happy feelings than negative ones, and to learn how they can cope with their negative feelings. Supporting children who are feeling an unpleasant or uncomfortable emotion will help to build their self-confidence and their ability to self-regulate when upset. Commenting on children's happy, joyful, proud, and excited emotions will increase their self-awareness of these pleasant moods. Children who can understand and regulate their own feelings will eventually be able to recognize and respond to feelings in others. Thus, emotion coaching leads to empathy.

Supporting children who are feeling an unpleasant or uncomfortable emotion will help to build their self-confidence.

Emotion coaching

Coaching Positive Emotions

Coaching positive or pleasant emotions is straightforward. Practice noticing and labeling each emotion that you see, along with the reason your child is feeling that way. For example, "You look like you are really excited about having ice cream for dessert tonight! Your whole body is bouncing!" "Your face looks so proud right now. It was hard to put that block in the hole and you got it in!" "You've got the biggest smile on your face. The dog's wagging tail is making you happy," "You shared with your friend and that makes her feel happy." If you provide the name for the emotion and some information about what lead to the emotion, you are helping your child link the feeling with the cause. You can also include information about the clues you used to guess the emotion (smile, bouncing body). This will help your child tune into physical cues about feelings. Try to coach as many positive feeling states as you can. If you pay attention to a range of positive feelings, your child will actually start to be in a positive feeling state more often. In other words, your attention to these feelings can make your child happier, more joyful, and more proud of himself. A good rule of thumb is to try to notice five times more positive than negative feelings in your child.

Your attention to these positive feelings can make your child happier, more joyful, and more proud of himself.

I notice and label emotions

Pair Negative Emotion Coaching with Coping Responses

Coaching your children's negative or unpleasant emotions is a little trickier because excessive attention to negative emotions can make your child more frustrated, angry, or sad. However, if done skillfully, coaching of unpleasant emotions can make your child feel validated, understood, and can help him regulate his mood and calm down and learn that these unpleasant feelings change with time. To do this it is important to pair your comments about your toddler's negative feelings with positive coping statements. For example, your toddler is having trouble getting his shoes on and you say, "That is frustrating, but you are staying so patient and you keep trying to get them on. I think you're going to do it." Or, your child is disappointed because he wanted to go to the park and something has come up that you can't take him. You say, "That must be very disappointing for you. I'm really sorry. Even though you are mad, you are staying calm. Let's think of something else to do now that will be fun and then we will feel happier." In this way, you avoid giving too much attention to negative behaviors, focus on a coping response to the negative feelings, and predict an eventual positive change in the negative feeling. This may even pre-empt a negative response, such as a temper tantrum. However, it is also possible that your child may be too dysregulated to listen to your coaching. If you have labeled the unpleasant emotion once and provided the coping strategy, and your child is crying hard or tantrumming, then it is a good idea to back off, ignore it and give him some space to calm down himself before talking again. Additional attention or talking during the tantrum will likely prolong the

Coaching of unpleasant emotions can make your child feel validated and understood.

fussing. When your child has finally calmed down, then you can label that emotion. "I'm proud of you. Your body is looking much calmer now. You really tried hard and now you are calm!"

TODDLER ALERT

Pay more attention to toddlers' positive emotions and coping behaviors, such as keeping hands to own body or trying again, than negative emotions and behaviors. If your toddler is tantrumming or completely dysregulated, and is in a safe place, it is a good idea to ignore this and wait until he calms down before commenting on his changing feelings. This is more likely to help him learn how to self-regulate, addresses his drive for independence and avoids reinforcing the negative or disruptive behavior.

Tailoring Emotion Coaching to Your Child's Temperament

Once you have learned how to generally coach children's emotions, your next task will be to learn to tailor your emotion coaching to the particular temperament or emotional needs of your child. Check the temperament questionnaire you completed in chapter one. Remember we talked about how every child is different. For example, a withdrawn, anxious, or fearful child will benefit from focused coaching when he takes risks. For example, the parent can say, "You are so brave, you tried something new," or "That was really courageous to invite him to play," "I could see it was scary to talk to that girl, but you did it and now you are enjoying playing together!" On the other hand, children who are angry and defiant will receive extra emotion coaching at times when they are calm, relaxed, joyful and agreeable. For example, the parent can say, "You seem happy and peaceful now. You went along with your friend's suggestion and it worked out well for you both." Children who are impulsive and inattentive will be coached especially when they are staying calm, patient, and able to wait and are thoughtful in their responses. Think about the emotion coaching in the next scenario of a mother with her three-year-old language-delayed son playing outside in a bucket of water with some rocks and some kitchen utensils.

Mother asks Kalani if he is going to cook something with his spoon. He stirs his hand in the water, and his mother asks him if it is cold. Then he wants to put his feet in the water and she prepares him for it by telling him it will be cold. As he puts his foot in the water, he slips and pulls his foot out looking scared and a little surprised. His mother gently holds onto him and says, "That is scary and cold." He tries again to put his foot back in the

Tailor your emotion coaching to the particular temperament or emotional needs of your child.

I practice emotion coaching

water. His mother comments, "You are brave and courageous. You keep trying." He asks for more water, which she gives to him, and he pours it in the water. He puts his foot in a third time and she asks him how it feels. When he doesn't answer she says, "It is slippery." They laugh together as she holds him, and she talks about how scary and slippery and fun it is in the water and how brave he is.

As demonstrated by this scenario, the mother supports Kalani's insecure feelings by holding him securely when he puts his foot in the water, giving him words to express his feelings, and pointing out how well he is managing this new experience. Her approach helps to build his self-confidence as well as his ability to self-regulate, stay calm and try again, even when the task is difficult.

Combine Emotion and Persistence Coaching

Remember persistence coaching from the prior chapter? Emotion coaching can often be combined with persistence coaching because tasks that require persistence can often be frustrating and difficult at first. However if a child persists, then proud feelings of accomplishment may result. Notice how the mother in this next example combines persistence and emotion coaching to help her three-year-old girl with a frustrating task of cutting and using large, sticky packing tape. The task is beyond the girl's developmental ability and could be quite frustrating. Let's see how this mother encourages her child's need for independence as she continues to try to do this difficult task herself.

Soleil is working hard on cutting some big sticky tape and her mother comments, "You are being very patient with the tape and now you have cut three pieces of tape." Soleil starts to cut again and asks her mother to hold the tape. Mother holds the tape for her and Soleil successfully cuts another piece of tape. Her mother smiles at her and appreciates her accomplishment and says, "You look proud of your cutting." As Soleil puts the tape on her picture, her mother comments, "You have been so focused on this work. Do you like this picture?" And when Soleil says yes, her mother says, "I am glad you like your picture, you have worked hard on it." Soleil cuts another piece of tape and she seems to be getting upset. Her mother asks, "Are you getting frustrated with the tape?" Soleil says "No" but looks more frustrated and asks her mother for help. Her mother acknowledges her feelings by saying, "It is frustrating when the tape gets stuck together. You're doing a great job of keeping your body calm even though you are frustrated. You keep working at it

Feelings of accomplishment

and are patient." Mother continues by saying, "You are working so diligently with the tape and you are feeling so…" The mother leaves a pause here so that Soleil has a chance to identify her own feeling.

Here is an example of how a mother is combining the persistence coaching discussed in Chapter 2 with the emotion coaching strategies. The mother effectively keeps her daughter working on this frustrating task by acknowledging the frustrating feelings but then moving on to her daughter's persistence at working hard, staying focused, and staying calm. The mother gives her just enough support to keep her daughter going without taking over the activity and doing it for her.

Emotion coaching can often be combined with persistence coaching.

Using Pretend Play to Promote Social and Emotional Skills

Pretend or imaginary play is a good way for parents to help their children practice both social and emotional skills by using all the coaching skills mentioned above: prompting, modeling, descriptive comments, and praise. For example, through the use of a puppet you can ask your child, "Will you play with me?" These are the friendly words a young child needs to learn to initiate an interaction with a peer. If your toddler ignores you, your puppet can ask again, showing how one can keep trying. Or, if this still doesn't work, your puppet can say, "I'm disappointed but I'll be patient and wait until you have finished with that and then maybe you will play with me." On the other hand, if your toddler agrees to let your puppet play with him you can reply, "Thank you. That makes me happy. You are a friend. What shall we do?" You can also engage in imaginary play by pretending to be a hungry horse or happy cow or grumpy pig, or by making the noise of a tired airplane or train. If your toddler is making play dough cookies, you can pretend they are real and say, "I'm hungry, can I have a taste of your green cookie?" If your child gives you a bite, pretend to eat to some and then comment on how good they taste. "I'm so happy to enjoy your delicious cookies! Thank you for being such a kind cook." With pretend phones you can make up imaginary calls. Using doll houses or Legos with figures (e.g., doctor, policeman) you can have a character pretend to be sick or model coming to the rescue when a house is burning down. By taking on the role of a character or action figure in pretend play, you are helping your children practice

Through the use of a puppet you can ask your child, "Will you play with me?"

social skills, express feelings with emotion language, and understand the emotions of another. It can be a powerful way to promote your children's imaginary worlds as well as to help them experience the perspective and feelings of another character. This is the beginning of empathy development.

Extending Coaching Skills to Other Times than Play

Social, emotional, academic, and persistence coaching is a way of communicating and interacting that you can use most any time during the day—such as during meal times, in the grocery store, in the car, at bed time, and during bath times. By using this coaching throughout the day you will be contributing to your child's optimal language, social and emotional development as well as strengthening your relationship. In the next example two parents are using child-centered social coaching during breakfast with their two-year-old daughter, Lia, and their four-year-old son Daniel. Think about what these children are learning.

Father praises Daniel for good eating. Lia is eating yogurt, and Father asks her, "Can I have a bite?" (Prompting a share.) She says, "No" and he responds humorously by saying, "No bite for Father?" Then she offers him a bite and he thanks her. (Praise for sharing.) She offers him several more spoonfuls and he eats them saying, "Thank you" each time she offers him a bite. (Modeling a polite response.) He praises her saying, "You're a good yogurt sharer." Then Daniel asks his father if he wants any of his eggs and Father eats some and praises him for sharing eggs. (Daniel has observed his little sister's sharing behavior and imitates it.). He says, "Wow sharing points all around." (Descriptive praise.) Mother comes in and says, "Food tastes better when you share it, don't you think?" and Father tells his wife that a lot of sharing has been going on that morning.

It is important to make meal times fun and enjoyable. This father is modeling enjoyment of food himself for his children as well as praising them for the social skill of sharing. He is child-centered allowing them to decide how much they will

It is important to make meal times fun and enjoyable.

eat. The breakfast time seems relaxed, low stress and a fun time for the family to be together. You can also use this social and emotion coaching during bath time or while you are taking a walk or stroll or are in the grocery store.

Next you will see an example of how the mother of the same children uses this coaching approach to promote her children's social behavior in the grocery store. Think what the children are learning.

Mother puts Daniel in the front of the grocery cart and Lia in the back. She offers Lia a bag to hold and asks if she wants to put the plums in the bag. (Prompts helping) Lia counts them as she puts the plums in her bag. Mother responds enthusiastically to her counting and suggests to Daniel, "Can you help Lia count the plums?" (Prompt) He responds by telling her he is so hungry he needs something. Mother continues to help her toddler count the plums in bag. (Notice she doesn't force Daniel to help.) Daniel asks if they can find some blueberries and looks for them on sale. Mother finds the blueberries and gives each child a blueberry for staying calm. (Labeling and reinforcing positive emotion.) She gives Daniel the blueberries to hold and he says, "I will be in charge of the blueberries." She replies, "Daniel, thanks for helping me." (She now has a chance to praise his helping behavior.) "Do you think you remember what other groceries we need?" (Another prompt.) He replies milk, yogurt and basil, fruit and vegetables. She replies, "You are a real helper and we are a team, I think we will remember everything. This is fun shopping with you." (More descriptive praise for his helping.)

Emotion Coaching helps children with the first steps toward empathy and self-regulation.

This mother uses social coaching to good effect in the grocery store. In the beginning her son is not responsive to her prompt for help. She lets this go and instead focuses on her daughter's helpfulness. Soon her son is offering to help and she gives him praise and attention which leads to his willingness to help again and he learns that this makes his mother happy.

To Sum Up...

When you play with your toddler using a toddler-directed approach coupled with social and emotion coaching you are modeling empathy and understanding. This type of coaching will help develop your toddler's specific social skills as well as emotional literacy. This will build your emotional relationship with your child and will set the stage for his social interactions with others. You are supporting your child's social and emotional brain development because having words to express feelings is the first step toward self-regulation and development of empathy. Understanding and using specific social skills such as asking, waiting, and sharing are core to successful friendships and relationships of all kinds. By scaffolding your child's negative feelings with emphases on coping responses (waiting patiently in contrast to the whining) and giving more focused attention to his positive feelings and coping strategies, you are helping him learn how to stay calm despite feelings of frustration. Moreover, social coaching helps your child learn how to develop positive relationships with peers through sharing, waiting, helping and taking turns. These friendly interactions will in turn lead to more positive feelings and self-confidence on the part of your child.

Positive attention

Points to Remember about
Promoting Your Toddler's Emotion Self-regulation Skills

• Try to understand what your toddler is feeling and wanting.

• Describe your toddler's feelings (don't ask him what he is feeling because he is unlikely to have the words to tell you).

• Label your toddler's positive feelings more often than his negative feelings.

• When naming negative feelings such as frustration or anger, point out the coping strategy your child is using: *"You look frustrated, but you are staying calm and trying again."*

• Praise your child's self-regulation skills such as staying calm, being patient, trying again when frustrated, waiting a turn, and using words.

I label positive feelings

• Support your toddler when he is frustrated, but recognize when he is too upset to listen and just needs space to calm down.

• Model and give your toddler the words to use to express his needs (e.g., You can say, "can I have the truck").

• Help your toddler learn ways to self-soothe such as using a pacifier or blanket or special stuffed animal.

• Praise and encourage your toddler when he stays calm in a frustrating situation.

• Cuddle and soothe your toddler when he is hurt or frightened. Stay calm yourself to provide extra reassurance.

Points to Remember about
Promoting Your Toddler's Social Competence

I model social skills

One-on-One Parent-Toddler

- During play, model social skills for your toddler such as offering to share, waiting, giving a compliment, taking turns, asking for help.
- Prompt your toddler to ask for help, take a turn, share something, or give a compliment and then praise if it occurs. Let it go if your toddler does not respond to your prompt.
- Praise your toddler any time s/he offers to share with you or help you.
- Participate in pretend and make-believe play with your child by using a doll, action figure, or puppet to model skills such as asking to play, offering to help, taking a turn, giving a compliment, calming down with a deep breath and waiting.
- Model and prompt your child with a suggestion of the appropriate words to use.
- Try to give enough help so children are successful but not so much help that you take over.

Peer Social Coaching

- Occasionally prompt your child to notice what another child is doing or to help him or her in some way.

- Help your toddler understand that when he shared, the other person felt happy so he can see the connection between his behavior and another's feelings.
- Encourage play dates with friends.
- Praise and encourage children's ideas and creativity; avoid criticism.
- Use descriptive comments instead of asking questions.
- Prompt, coach, and praise children's friendly behaviors whenever you see them (e.g., sharing, helping, taking turns, being polite).
- Laugh and have fun.

I help my toddler see the connections between behavior and another's feelings

Social & Emotional Developmental Milestones
25–30 MONTHS

- Talks about self ("me") (25 months)
- Uses pronouns (e.g., I, me, you) (26 months)
- Uses 3-word sentences (25 months)
- Speaks clearly (27 months)
- Can answer some questions (26 months)
- Vocabulary increases to 300 words (30 months)
- Understands descriptions (28 months)
- Starts to recognize ABCs
- Brushes teeth with help (29-30 months)
- Aware of need to pee or poop (25-30 months)
- Names a color (30 months)

Learning sentences

Physical Developmental Milestones
25–30 MONTHS

- Can walk downstairs (25 months)
- Learns to jump (25 months)
- Washes and dries own hands (26 months)
- Draws a circle (30 months)
- Puts on shirt (30-32 months)

I monitor milestones

EMOTION JOURNAL
PARENTS AS "EMOTION COACHES"

Describing children's feelings is a powerful way to strengthen your child's emotional literacy. Once children have emotion language, they will be able to better regulate their own emotions because they can tell you how they feel. The following is a list of emotions that can be commented upon when playing with a child. Use this checklist to practice describing your child's emotions and write down your examples on the blank journal page. Notice what type of emotions you tend to focus on.

Feelings/Emotional Literacy

happy	patient
frustrated	funny
calm	jealous
proud	forgiving
excited	caring
pleased	curious
sad	angry
helpful	mad
worried	interested
confident	embarrassed
fearful	brave

EXAMPLES OF EMOTION COACHING

- "That is frustrating, and you are staying calm and trying to do that again."

- "You look proud of that drawing."

- "You seem confident when reading that story."

- "You are so patient. Even though it fell down twice, you just keep trying to see how you can make it taller. You must feel pleased with yourself for being so patient."

- "You look like you are having fun playing with your friend, and he looks like he enjoys doing this with you."

- "You are so curious. You are trying out every way you think that can go together."

- "You are forgiving of your friend because you know it was a mistake."

Modeling Feeling Talk and Sharing Feelings

- "I am proud of you for solving that problem."

- "I am really having fun playing with you."

- "I was nervous it would fall down, but you were careful and patient, and your plan worked."

I model positive feelings talk

SOCIAL SKILLS JOURNAL
PARENTS AS "SOCIAL SKILLS COACHES"

Describing and prompting children's friendly behaviors is a powerful way to strengthen children's social skills. Social skills are the first steps to making lasting friendships. The following is a list of social skills that you can comment on when playing with your child or when your child is playing with a friend. Use this checklist to practice your social skills coaching and write down some examples on the blank journal page. Think about what social skills you want to encourage in your child.

Social/Friendship Skills

helping

sharing

teamwork

using a friendly voice (quiet, polite)

listening to what a friend says

taking turns

asking

trading

waiting

agreeing with a friend's suggestion

making a suggestion

asking permission to use
  something a friend has

problem solving

cooperating

being generous

including others

apologizing

giving a compliment

using soft, gentle touch

EXAMPLES OF SOCIAL COACHING

- "That's so friendly. You are sharing your blocks with your friend and waiting your turn."
- You are both working together and helping each other like a team."
- You listened to your friend's request and followed his suggestion. That is very friendly."
- You waited and asked first if you could use that. Your friend listened to you and shared.
- You are taking turns. That's what good friends do for each other."
- You made a friendly suggestion and your friend is doing what you suggested. That is so friendly."
- "You are helping your friend build his tower. That is team work."
- "You are being cooperative by sharing."
- "You both solved the problem of how to put those blocks together. That was a great solution."

I encourage social skills

Prompting
- "Look at what your friend has made. Do you think you can give him a compliment?" (praise child if s/he tries to give a compliment)
- "You did that by accident. Do you think you can say you are sorry to your friend?" (praise if s/he tries to apologize)

Modeling Friendly Behavior

• Parents can model waiting, taking turns, helping, and complimenting, which also teach children these social skills.

Remember to be realistic about what is developmentally appropriate to expect for toddlers!

Model friendly behavior

Parents' Viewpoint
MY SOCIAL SKILLS AND EMOTION COACHING JOURNAL

Write here your favorite social and emotion coaching statements.

Toddler's Viewpoint
THINGS I CAN DO (25–30 months)

Activity	Date	Observations/Comments
I can talk about myself		
I speak pretty well	Yes	
I am starting to recognize ABCs	Yes	
I can brush my teeth with help	yes	
I am aware when I need to pee or poo	Yes	
I can name a color	No/yes	

Toddler's Viewpoint
THINGS I CAN DO (25–30 months)

Activity	Date	Observations/Comments

I can walk downstairs

Yes

I am learning to jump

Know

I like to run

Know

I love to act out songs
and do finger plays

Yes

I love sandboxes with water

Yes

I love things that can be taken
apart and put back together

Yes

Toddler's Viewpoint
THINGS I CAN DO (25–30 months)

Activity	Date	Observations/Comments
I can wash and dry my own hands		
wash hands		
I can draw a circle		
yes		
I can put on a shirt by myself		
yes backw		
My attention span is short		
yes		
I am beginning to involve others in pretend play		
yes		
I love to play with dolls, dress-up clothes, toy phones, forts		
yes		

Toddler's Viewpoint
THINGS I CAN DO (25–30 months)

Activity	Date	Observations/Comments
I have trouble knowing what is real and what is pretend	No	
I can express my feelings	yes	
I love painting, crayons, and chalk	yes	
I can sing simple songs	yes	
I like to be given choices	No but love's to help	

MY TODDLER'S PICTURE
(25–30 months)

CHAPTER 4

Positive Attention, Encouragement and Praise

Introduction

In earlier chapters we have talked about how parental toddler-directed play, and academic, persistence, and social-emotion coaching are powerful ways of promoting your toddler's cooperative social behaviors, emotional regulation, language skills, preschool readiness, and parent-child bonding. Parental praise, encouragement and spontaneous incentives or celebrations are the next two levels in the parenting pyramid and can also be used to nurture toddlers through the many small steps it takes for them to master new social skills. Unfortunately, without realizing it, many parents spend more time correcting and criticizing toddlers than praising them. While it may seem that corrections and lectures about negative behavior should teach your toddler to behave better, your scolding probably has just the opposite effect. It is likely to make your child more resistant to your efforts and threaten your relationship building.

Paradoxically, negative attention and corrections that are given when children are misbehaving actually strengthen the brain pathways to negative behavior.

Instead you want to strengthen brain pathways to positive behaviors by striving to have your coaching statements and praise out-number your correcting statements by at least 10 to one. In other words, you will spend more time praising, describing, and strengthening the "positive opposite" behaviors than the negative ones. In this chapter we are going to focus on the added benefit of praise and how parents can use praise effectively during the toddler period. Actually praise is a component of the coaching we talked about earlier, but it makes your approval more explicitly apparent than a coaching statement. For example, you might coach a social behavior like sharing by saying, "I see that you just shared the block with your sister." To turn this into coached praise, you might add the words, "I'm really pleased that you were so generous." Thus, praise is parental verbal approval that is combined with coaching to indicate your pleasure in observing your toddler's particular behaviors or interactions.

Parents often overlook the importance of using praise and other social rewards such as positive attention, smiles, and hugs with their children. Some believe children should behave appropriately without adult intervention, and that praise should be reserved for exceptionally good behavior or outstanding performances. In many cases, parents don't praise their children when they are playing quietly or following

Spend more time praising, describing, and strengthening the "positive opposite" behaviors than the negative ones.

Praising

their directions or waiting for something or eating healthy foods. Research indicates, however, that a lack of praise and attention for appropriate child behaviors can actually lead to an increase in misbehavior because inappropriate behaviors are one way children can be sure to get your attention! In fact, praise and encouragement can be used to guide children through the many small steps it takes to master new skills, to help them develop a positive self-image, and to provide the motivation they need to stay with a difficult task. Unlike tangible rewards such as money or privileges, there can be an almost endless "supply" of praise and other social rewards. It takes very little time to encourage positive behaviors in children. A simple statement such as, "I like the way you are playing quietly—what a patient girl!" or a well-timed hug is all that is required.

While some parents believe they should not praise their children or save it for outstanding performance, many others simply do not know how or when to give praise and encouragement. Perhaps they experienced little or no praise themselves when they were young and are unaccustomed to hearing praise, the words may seem awkward and artificial. Or, perhaps they don't know what child behaviors justify a praise response. Still other parents may feel their child is so oppositional, defiant or impulsive that they can find nothing to praise or resist giving it. They may be so stressed by these misbehaviors that they cannot see praiseworthy behaviors nor do they think their child deserves praise even when the positive behaviors do occur. Yet, parents and other adults can learn effective praise and encouragement skills, and when they do, they find that using social rewards and providing positive attention has

It takes very little time to encourage positive behaviors in children.

a dramatic impact in improving their children's behavior and feelings as well as their relationship. Moreover, they are teaching their children, through their modeling, how to be positive and encouraging with others.

Parents who don't praise their children often don't praise themselves, either. If they listened to their internal self-talk, they would find that they are rarely or never saying things to themselves like, "You're doing a good job of disciplining Johnny," or "You handled that conflict calmly and rationally," or "You've been very patient in this situation." Instead, they are quick to criticize themselves for every flaw or mistake they make. These parents can also learn how to stop these negative thoughts and focus instead on "positive opposite" thoughts, to self-praise by focusing on their successes and solutions to problems rather than their mistakes and to create positive experiences for themselves. When they do this, they are then more likely to do the same for their children.

In the first part of this chapter, we will discuss some of the erroneous objections parents raise to praising children, then we will discuss effective and ineffective ways to praise children and themselves and finally about specific behaviors to target for praise during the toddler developmental period.

> Parents who don't praise their children often don't praise themselves, either.

Positive tone of voice

Objections to Praise

Here are some common questions or concerns that parents ask about praise.

Should children know how to behave?

"My child should know how to behave. Surely I don't need to praise her for everyday things like getting dressed or sharing toys or eating or sitting in her chair?"

Expecting a child to function without encouragement and praise is unrealistic. Think about how hard it is for a toddler to learn how to put on a shirt or her shoes by herself, or sit still in a chair? Rules or statements about expected behavior are not sufficient for motivating her behavior. The only way your toddler learns to engage in a particular behavior is by supporting and scaffolding that positive behavior through your assistance, encouragement and praise. When this happens, the behavior is more likely to occur again. If it is ignored, it is less likely your toddler will make the effort to try again in the future. Consequently, no positive social behavior should be taken for granted or it will soon disappear.

> Expecting a child to function without encouragement and praise is unrealistic.

Does praise spoil children?

"Isn't there a danger of spoiling my toddler with praise? Won't she learn to cooperate only for the sake of some external reward or adult approval?"

If there are any examples of children who have developed behavior problems as a result of receiving too much praise, they are rare indeed. The truth is that children are not spoiled by praise, nor do they learn to work only for external approval or rewards. In fact, the opposite is true: children who will work only for external attention or rewards tend to be those who receive little praise or reinforcement from adults. They are usually receiving a great number of commands and criticisms and few praises. As a result, their self-esteem is so low that they are always seeking others' approval; or they demand a reward before complying with requests.

Children who receive a lot of encouragement and positive approval from their parents develop increased self-esteem.

On the other hand, children who receive a lot of coaching, encouragement and positive approval from their parents develop increased self-esteem. This positive self-esteem eventually makes them less dependent on approval from adults and external rewards; they are more able to provide themselves with positive feedback. Moreover, children who receive positive messages about themselves are also more likely to praise others, and this can have far-reaching effects. The principle that operates here is, "you get what you give." Research indicates that children who give many positive statements to others in school are popular and get many positive statements from others, which in turn bolsters their self-esteem. So remember: children imitate or model what they see and hear. If they receive frequent positive messages from their parents, they are more likely to internalize this form of thinking and use it in positive self-talk to bolster their own confidence and with the people around them. Of course, the opposite is also true. If parents are negative and critical, their children will model this behavior and negative self-talk as well.

Isn't there a difference between encouragement and praise?

"I make a point of encouraging my child, isn't that enough?"

Some parents believe that they should encourage their children but not praise them. Often these are the same parents who worry about spoiling or ending up with children who work only for external rewards. They

Give encouragement and praise as frequently as you notice the positive behaviors.

make supportive comments, but avoid any statements that sound like praise. This causes them to continue to edit what they say, out of concern that their encouragement is really praise. This creates an unnecessary complication, since children aren't likely to notice the difference. Don't worry about how you are giving a positive statement, simply give encouragement and praise as frequently as you notice the positive behaviors. In fact, effective praise given with a coaching statement is really the same thing as encouragement.

Should praise be saved for really outstanding performances?

"I prefer to save my praise for something that's really worth praising —such as being toilet trained, sleeping in her own bed all night, being dressed and ready for day care on time. Doesn't this help a child reach for the top?"

The problem with this approach is that no one—child or adult—achieves perfection without completing many steps along the way. A parent's focus should be on the child's process of trying to use the toilet, or putting on her own shoes or getting dressed. Otherwise, the opportunity to praise may never come up: children with parents who reserve their praise for perfection usually give up trying before they have reached it.

Therefore, instead of hoarding praises, practice praising your child for a small positive behavior. Notice when she is sitting in her chair, asking to go to the toilet, having a dry night in bed, using her words to ask for what she wants, and starting to follow a direction. Don't take these behaviors for granted, praise them. If you focus on the fact that your child is trying to use the toilet, or put on her shoes, or saying please, you will be gradually shaping her behavior in the desired direction. In other words, remember to praise the process of trying to achieve, not just the achievement.

The other thing to keep in mind is what behavior is developmentally appropriate for toddlers and to be sure that unrealistic expectations aren't contributing to your frustration and a reluctance to praise. All the above tasks (toilet training, sleeping in own bed, getting dressed alone) are developmental milestones for the toddler years and will take a long time to become independent habits. It's your job to support your toddler during the learning process and your praise and encouragement will help do this. In addition, did you know that, on average, toddlers are disobedient or noncompliant about 80-90% of the time and that most toddlers react to disappointment with some aggression. Moreover, their ability to pay attention, stay still, understand verbal instructions or keep their hands to themselves depends in part on their individual temperament and neurological development. As a parent, you will be helping your child to

Praise positive behaviors

I praise the process of achieving

become more cooperative, compliant, and self-controlled, but this will only happen in small stages as your child is developmentally ready. Again, your praise will be crucial every step of the way.

Every toddler is different in this regard and will need different levels of attention and praise for different behaviors. Review the temperament questionnaire you completed in chapter 1. Is your toddler impulsive or explosive by nature, does she have trouble sitting still, is she very shy, or very sensitive to change? You can begin to tailor your praise to address specific goals for your child. You may start to look for any time your impulsive child is walking quietly, sitting calmly, or being patient and give her praise for these behaviors. Or you may look for times when your fearful child is brave, independent, or copes with change and encourage these behaviors.

Praise positive behaviors

Avoid Combining Praise with Put-Downs

"I tease my kids quite a bit when they do something well — is there a problem with this?"

Some people give praise and, without realizing it, they contradict it by being sarcastic or combining it with a punisher. This is one of the most disruptive things a parent can do in the reinforcement process. In particular, seeing their children do something they haven't done before seems to tempt some parents to make a sarcastic or critical remark about the new behavior. For example, a father may say to his three-year old son, "Tony I can't believe you didn't wet your bed last night." Or a mother may say, "Lee, you actually used the toilet and not your diaper, but you just went pee. Next time try to go poop too."

In these examples, the parents may feel they have praised their children's efforts but they have actually undermined their praise by adding some sense of discouragement or disbelief in them and some implied criticism or disapproval. Perhaps they think they

Every toddler is different and will need different levels of attention and praise.

have praised, but their children will tend to hear the parents' criticisms, not the praise. That is, they will hear that they didn't do a good enough job. If you seem discouraged or discouraging, as these parents did, your child will stop trying. When you give praise, it should be clear and unequivocal, without reminders of prior failures or less-than-perfect performance. Don't contaminate your praise.

When you give praise, it should be clear and unequivocal, without reminders of prior failures.

Does the behavior have to change before praise is given?

"My child has been consistently naughty. She is nothing but trouble. I am always yelling at her to pay attention and I can't start to praise her until she changes her ways."

The danger here is that you could be involved in a stalemate situation. It is unlikely that the child is going to be able to initiate a behavior change. But someone has to stop the negative interactions, and so this must be the parent.

Sam, a father, provides a good example of the wrong approach. Sam is constantly irritated by the fact that his two-year-old son, Steve, doesn't listen or pay attention to him and runs away whenever he asks him to do something. Sam gets cross with Steve frequently because of his impulsivity. As a result, Sam is never in a mood to notice that, at times, Steve does play quietly with his Legos and sometimes follows his instructions. If this were pointed out to him, Sam would likely say "So what?" because he is totally focused on Steve not listening and being disobedient. Unfortunately, this means that Steve can only access his father's attention by being noncompliant and impulsive.

Parents like Sam must learn to shift their focus to the positive things their children are doing and to praise them for their efforts. Then children will likely repeat and expand these positive behaviors. In other words, only if parents take the responsibility for changing first is there the likelihood of positive changes in the relationship. This same principle is true of any relationship — with spouses, older children, or working colleagues. If one becomes obstinate and refuses to make a positive change in one's own behavior, the status quo is maintained and the relationship is unlikely to improve.

I look for positive behaviors

Is praise manipulative and phony?

"Isn't it rather manipulative to use praise to bring about a particular behavior in my child? If I make a conscious effort to praise her, I just end up feeling phony."

The word manipulative implies that a parent is contriving secretly to bring about some desired behavior against the child's wishes. In fact, the purpose of praise is to enhance and increase positive behavior with the child's knowledge. Praise that is clearly described brings out the best behavior in children because they learn what is expected of them. Praise may seem "phony" when it is first used — any new behavior feels awkward in the beginning. This is a natural reaction and is to be expected. But remember, the more you use praise, the more natural it will feel.

Model self-praise

Do some parents find it harder than others to praise their children?

"It's not that I have any real objection to praising my child, I can see its value, but it just isn't something that comes naturally to me and so I don't do it because it isn't me."

Very often parents who find praise "unnatural" are people who were never praised as children and who don't praise themselves. They are often very critical of themselves for their mistakes, conflicts, and difficulties. They may tell their children and other family members about things in

I DID A GOOD JOB FIXING THAT!

their life they are discouraged with or their problems, but rarely do they mention their successes at home or at work.

Such parents do not model self-praise for their children. If they listened to their internal self-talk, they would find that they are not saying things like, "I did a good job on my assignment at work," or "That was a tough situation but I think I handled it well and was patient," or "That casserole I made tonight tasted good." Instead, they are quick to criticize themselves for every flaw. They must learn to speak to themselves in positive statements and to create positive experiences for themselves. They will then be able to do that for their children. By modeling self-praise for your children, you are teaching them how to internalize positive self-talk. This is important because they are learning how to self-evaluate and internalize their own self-motivation strategies.

What if a parent forgets to praise?

"Sometimes I forget to praise and do it later — is there a problem with this?"

Sometimes praise is given hours or even days after the positive behavior has occurred. For adults and teenagers, who are able to connect their past actions with the praise, delayed praise will likely still have meaning. However, young children will be unable to link the praise with their past behavior. For toddlers and preschoolers the most effective praise is that which is given immediately after the positive behavior. This means that if you are trying to encourage a new behavior, you should watch for every occasion when your child attempts the behavior. You should praise as soon as your child begins to perform the desired behavior, rather than waiting for the clothes to be put on perfectly or the toys all put away before praising. The praise should be frequent and consistent in the beginning, and then gradually it can be replaced by more intermittent praise.

What about when the praise seems to disrupt the play?

"When I go in and tell him he is playing well with his sister, they stop playing and start arguing. I feel I should have just left them alone — they were doing so well." "My child was building a Lego tower quietly by himself. When I praised him for working hard, he followed me into the kitchen asking me to help. We were both better off before I praised."

It's important to praise your child (or children) who are playing independently and quietly because this conveys the message that cooperation and independence are desirable behaviors! However, at times, going into a room to praise children for their quiet, cooperative play may have the unwanted consequence of disrupting the play. Sometimes the children will stop playing and ask the parent to stay and play. Other times the interruption may even seem to precipitate an argument between siblings. This kind of response is most common when parents first start to praise independent play. The praise may be new for the children, and parents' positive enthusiasm can make children want to spend more time playing with them. Parent attention can also upset the balance between siblings. Nonetheless, as children get used to you peeking in their rooms to notice how they are playing, it will become less disruptive and your children will know you feel good about their independent and cooperative play. This will be particularly true if there are plenty of other times during the day when you are playing directly with them with your full attention.

Praise independent play

You might ask, "Why praise children when they are playing quietly? If observing them and commenting is disruptive, why not leave them alone?" Think about what happens if you don't

As children get used to you peeking in their rooms to notice how they are playing, it will become less disruptive.

comment on the quiet, positive play. Sooner or later your child or children will get bored with the activity and will begin to pester you or sibling conflict will erupt. At this point, you will be forced to respond. However, instead of giving your attention to the quiet positive behavior, you will be giving attention to the disruptive behavior, thereby reinforcing it. Your children will learn that the way to get

you involved is to bother you or to be disruptive—not the message or the brain connections that you would like them to learn or you want to strengthen.

What about when a child rejects praise?

"Whenever I try to praise my child, she throws it back in my face. She never seems to believe what I say. It's almost as if she doesn't want me to praise her."

Temperamentally difficult and aggressive children can be hard to praise. Their behavior often makes parents angry and undermines their desire to be positive. To make matters more difficult, such children may seem to ignore parental praise when it is given to them as if they don't care or don't hear it. It is possible they have internalized a negative self-concept because of prior experiences and, when parents present them with an alternative, positive view of themselves, they may find this image difficult to accept and cling to their familiar negative self-image. It is also possible that they may not be understanding that they are receiving praise because they are not paying attention or processing the verbal information.

While "temperamentally difficult" children who are very active, impulsive, inattentive and aggressive are hard to praise and reward, they need it even more than other children. Their parents must constantly look for positive behaviors that they can praise in an effective way until their children begin to internalize some positive self-concepts. At that point they will no longer have a need to reject praise in order to maintain their poor self-image. However, this is easier said than done. It can be incredibly difficult for parents to continue to be positive with a difficult child who ignores or even rejects their praise and their efforts to break a stalemate but it is well worth the effort.

Comment on quiet, positive play

Making Praise More Effective

It sometimes happens that parents praise their children in ineffective ways or miss opportunities to praise particular behaviors they want to see more of. Here are some ways to maximize your effectiveness at promoting your child's social, emotional, and academic brain development using effective praise methods.

Be Specific and Label Positive Behaviors

Vague praise is often given quickly in a chain, with one comment following another. It is nonspecific, neutral and unlabeled. For example, you might say, "Good job... good boy... great...good...fine..." Unfortunately, these statements do not describe the behavior you are trying to praise and the toddler does not understand what the parent is focusing on.

It is more effective to give praises that are labeled.

It is more effective to give praises that are labeled. Labeled praise describes the particular behavior that you like. Instead of saying "Good girl," or "Good job," you would say, "I love the way you are being so patient. You are sitting so quietly in your chair while I get your cereal," or "I'm pleased that you said thank you, that is so friendly and polite," or "Good boy for picking up those blocks when I asked. That is very helpful." This description of the positive behaviors will help your child understand exactly what prosocial behaviors are important to you. In essence you are combining your social or emotional coaching statements with your positive evaluation of your child's behavior and how it has made you feel.

Praise Appropriately

It is critical that praise be contingent on your child's appropriate behavior. Praise for sharing should occur at the time when your child is actually sharing a toy with her little brother. However, if the children are behaving inappropriately it is better to ignore whatever positive aspect there might be to their behavior rather than try to give some form of praise. For example, it would not be appropriate to praise Sarah for sharing her crayons with Danny when they have been using them to scribble all over the wall. Giving phony praise when a child is behaving inappropriately is misleading and confusing. Wait for your toddler to do something more constructive and then praise that positive behavior.

Show Enthusiasm

Some praise is ineffective because it is boring, offered in dull tones, with no smiles or eye contact. The same words may be repeated over and over again in a flat, unenthusiastic voice. Such praise is not reinforcing to children and in particular, won't be

understood by inattentive toddlers who are easily distracted by other more interesting and competing activities.

The impact of a praise statement can be increased by using nonverbal methods of conveying enthusiasm. Smile at your child, greet her with warmth in your eyes or give her a pat on the back. The praise should be stated with energy, care and sincerity. Words thrown over the shoulder in a careless fashion will be lost on the child.

Remember children who are inattentive, impulsive, and distracted will be most likely to miss praise that is delivered in a neutral voice or a vague way. These children, in particular, need praise that is underscored by means of an enthusiastic tone of voice, clear descriptions (labeling) of the positive behaviors, positive facial expressions and positive touch.

TODDLER ALERT

If giving praise is difficult for you and you are not used to it, it will sound somewhat artificial or boring in the beginning. This is to be expected. The genuine positive feeling will come as you use praise more and more often and see its effect on your child.

I use an enthusiastic voice

A few phrases to help you get started...
- • I like it when you...
- • You're putting away the blocks just like Mommy asked you to do. You are such a great helper.
- • You are listening and minding Daddy so well.
- • Mommy's very proud of you for...
- • Look how well he/she did at…
- • Beautiful! Awesome! Gorgeous! Tremendous!
- • Wow, what a wonderful job you've done of...
- • You're such a good friend for...
- • What a nice job of...
- • Hey, you are really patient, you...
- • Pat yourself on the back for...
- • You must feel proud of yourself for...

Praise with clear labels

Remember to combine physical rewards with verbal...
- • A pat on the arm or shoulder
- • A hug
- ✗ Head rubbing
- • Squeezing the arm or waist
- • Giving a kiss

Keep Your Praise Pure

Remember the pitfall above of combining praise with a put-down, a correction or sarcasm?

For example, a father may say to his children, "Tony and Angie, you both came to the table the first time I asked you. That's great. But next time how about washing your face and hands first." Or a mother may say, "Lee, I'm glad you're making your bed, but why can't you do it every morning?"

Keep your praise pure and focus on what they DID DO well and not on what they didn't do.

Remember that it is important to emphasize the positive aspects of your child's behavior. If you seem discouraged or discouraging, as did the parents above, your child will stop trying. When you praise, you should be clear and unequivocal without reminders of prior failures or less than perfect performance. Keep your praise pure and focus on what they DID DO well and not on what they didn't do.

Praise Immediately

Sometimes praise is given hours or even days after the positive behavior has occurred. For instance, a mother may mention that she appreciated her daughter wiping the table or putting her plate in the sink a few hours after it happened. Unfortunately, praise loses its reinforcing value with time and tends to sound more artificial.

While delayed praise is better than no praise, the most effective praise for teaching a toddler the desired behavior is that which is given within five seconds of the positive behavior. This means that if you're trying to encourage a new behavior, you should watch for every time your children share, comply with a request, or try to put on their clothes.

Don't wait for the clothes to be put on perfectly or the toys all put away before praising. Praise your children as soon as they begin to perform the desired behavior. Praise them for their efforts not just the end result. The praise should be frequent and consistent in the beginning, and then gradually it can be replaced by more intermittent praise.

Behavior Doesn't Have to Be Perfect to Deserve Recognition

Behavior doesn't have to be perfect to deserve your praise or positive attention. In fact, when children are first attempting a new behavior, they need to be reinforced for each small step toward the goal. If they have to wait until they have mastered the new behavior before receiving praise, they may give up altogether. Praising a child for small steps along the way reinforces children for their efforts and learning. This process, known as "shaping," sets children up for success.

Praise them for their efforts not just the end result.

Encourage Children to Praise Themselves and Others

Ultimately, we want children to learn to praise others, for this is a skill that will help them build positive relationships with other children. We also want them to learn to praise themselves, for this will help them attempt and persist with difficult tasks. Parents can help their children learn how to recognize their own feelings of accomplishment by the way they phrase the praise. For example, statements such as, " You

must feel proud of yourself for getting dressed all by yourself. Give yourself a pat on the back" focuses on the child's own positive recognition of her work. Parents can also prompt their children to give compliments to others and then praise them for this friendly behavior. For example, "Lizzie, look at the great castle your friend has built. Can you tell her, 'I like it'?" Then when she gives her friend a compliment the parent can praise her, "that was really friendly and it looks like Lizzie feels happy."

Praising a child for small steps along the way reinforces children for their efforts.

Behaviors To Praise

Toddler Independence

Remember that one of toddlers' developmental tasks is the drive to explore and to begin to experience themselves as autonomous people. Often they strive for independence before they are fully developmentally ready or capable of doing the task alone. For example, the toddler who wants to use the toilet all by herself but still needs some parental help with cleaning herself. Parents can look for opportunities to praise their toddler's appropriate efforts to be independent while at the same time giving them adequate support to be successful and safe. Take the toddler who wants to drink from a big cup or to use a fork to eat before she is able to manipulate them safely. In this case, the parent might provide a special tippy cup with a handle that gives her control over the cup while at the same time assuring the milk won't land on the floor.

The trick is to look for opportunities to give your toddler some legitimate control and choices and for you to praise her efforts to be independent. When this happens your child won't have to resort to inappropriate ways of getting control. See how the mother of two-year-old Lia tries to do this in the following examples.

Lia's mother offers to cut her eggs for her at breakfast but Lia wants to do it herself and grabs the knife from her mother. Lia tries to cut her own egg and her mother replies, "You are being such a big girl cutting your own egg." She avoids criticizing her for grabbing the knife and focuses instead on her independent effort to feed herself. She stays close by to assure she is safe (the knife is not sharp).

When Lia wants to choose what she wears to day care, her mother lets her do this, despite the fact that nothing matches and she puts her bathing suit under her dress. Her mother praises her by saying, "You picked out your own outfit today, and got dressed all by yourself."

This mother has made the decision to honor her daughter's need for independence in eating and dressing. She monitors Lia's behavior to keep her safe, and gives up some control when Lia chooses an unusual outfit. Think about times when you can let your toddler make her own decisions or exercise some control. For example, give your daughter a choice of what to wear or what to eat, or what play activity she wants to do and then praise this independent behavior. Giving your toddler some control or choices at times will help increase compliance at times when you must set important rules, such as sitting in a car seat, going to bed, getting out of the house for daycare. In a sense, when you cooperate with your child's wishes, you are modeling compliance. You might even comment to your toddler as you do this: "You know, you have a good idea. I will listen and will cooperate with you."

Give your toddler choices

Meal Time Manners

Mealtimes are a good place to practice social coaching, encouragement, and praise. In the next scenario, think about what behaviors the father is praising and what makes his praise effective.

Father is sitting at the table with his two children and they are all having breakfast together. Lia, two-years-old, and Daniel, four-years-old, are sitting on either side of their father. Father looks at Lia and comments positively, "You're eating yummy eggs with your fork." Daniel copies his father's comment saying, "Eating with a fork" and takes a bite of his own eggs. Father asks Daniel if he wants yogurt and Daniel says, "No thanks." Father praises this polite response, saying, "That was a polite way to say 'no'." Father suggests that Daniel put his napkin in his lap. Daniel agrees saying, "I was just about to do that." Father thanks him for remembering. Daniel offers his father a bite of his egg and father replies, "Thank you for sharing your egg with me." They have a conversation about what will happen

at day care that day while they eat breakfast. Father praises both children by saying, "Wow you guys are good breakfast eaters." Lia asks her father, "Napkin please" and father praises her saying, "What a polite talker" and gives her the napkin. She wipes her mouth and he praises her again, "Good wiping and using your napkin."

In this scenario the father gives attention and praise to both children for eating, good manners, sharing, polite language, and Daniel's compliance to the request to use his napkin. The father's praise is frequent, specific, clear, and immediate. Both children are learning from the praise; Daniel repeats his father's comment to Lia about eating eggs and Lia wants to use her napkin after Daniel is praised for using his. All of this attention, coaching, and praise is teaching them about appropriate mealtime behaviors and manners. By eating breakfast with his children and talking with them about their day, this father is also reinforcing the importance of their meal times together and their social conversations. Think about the kinds of meal time behaviors you want to encourage and praise and why having mealtimes together is such a valuable time for families.

Sharing

Toddler-hood is the age of "mine mine mine." Remember that young toddlers are not developmentally ready to share with others since they are so focused on their individual sense of autonomy. However, parents can begin to help toddlers to understand what it means to share by praising it every time it occurs spontaneously. For

example, you might ask your toddler for a bite of one of her crackers, and if she offers you a cracker say, "Wow that was so friendly to share one of your crackers with me, thank you." Or, you might offer to share your egg, "I'm going to be friendly and share my egg with you." In this way you are modeling and labeling the behavior you want them to learn. In this way your young toddler will begin to learn these social skills. By the age of three, some children begin to emerge from the "mine" stage, and will be able to share some of the time, with your support and encouragement.

> Parents can begin to help toddlers to understand what it means to share by praising it every time it occurs.

TODDLER ALERT

Remember, though, that three- to five-year-olds still have trouble sharing at least some of the time, so be patient with the process as your toddler starts to learn what it means to be generous or to share.

Helping and Waiting

In the next scenario notice what behaviors this mother praises. Think about what makes her praise effective.

Mother, Lia, and Daniel are walking home from the grocery store and the blueberries fall out of her shopping bag onto the sidewalk. The mother asks Daniel to help her pick them up. He immediately starts picking them up. His mother says "Thank you for helping!" Next Daniel starts to eat some of the blueberries. Mother replies, "You can't eat them now because they are dirty." Daniel stops eating them and she says, "That was good listening!" Next mother turns to Lia, who is waiting in the stroller, saying, " Thank you for being so calm while you are waiting. I will give you and Daniel a bowl of blueberries when we get home, after I have washed them." She praises Daniel again, "Thanks for all the help you have given me to clean up all these blueberries." Next she praises Lia again for waiting.

This mother's praise is effective because it is labeled. She praises behaviors that can be difficult for toddlers such as waiting, helping, listening to her request, and staying calm. She combines her praise with information about when they will be able to eat the blueberries and provides clear reasons for her request not to eat them now (the blueberries are dirty). She helps both children feel valuable by emphasizing Lia's patience and Daniel's cooperation. These are important behaviors to praise during the toddler and preschool age period.

Give effective praise

A few toddler behaviors that are important to praise and encourage...
- Talking with a friendly voice
- Using words to ask for what they want
- Listening to parent requests
- Complying with parental requests
- Eating with spoon or fork
- Going to bed after begin asked
- Playing quietly
- Sponging the table
- Taking breakfast plate to kitchen sink
- Putting things in garbage
- Hanging up coat on hanger or leaving in specified place
- Using 'walking feet' in house (not running)
- Letting a parent know about a soiled diaper
- Sitting on the toilet
- Peeing or pooping in the toilet
- Getting up promptly in the morning
- Making it through the night without wetting the bed
- Helping make the bed
- Picking up clothes
- Putting toys away
- Talking quietly
- Reading or looking at a book
- Getting dressed
- Being friendly
- Being patient or staying calm
- Being kind to another child or adult

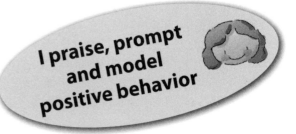
I praise, prompt and model positive behavior

Patience During Phone Calls

Often parents of toddlers find it difficult to talk on the phone. Phone calls are hard for toddlers because parents are withdrawing attention from them and giving it to someone else. Toddlers are curious to know what the phone call is all about. Parents can help train their children to wait quietly during a phone call by praising their efforts to entertain themselves. Look at all the strategies the mother uses in the next scenario.

Mother tells her 18-month old daughter Kayla and her toddler friend Jolie that she is going to be on the phone. She tells them she wants them to play quietly and gives them a book, blocks, and clock to play with. The girls start to play and mother makes her phone call to set up a play date.

Mother talks for 1-2 minutes and then interrupts her call to thank and praise the children for playing so quietly. "Wow you children are being so quiet and friendly. That is very helpful, thank you." At the end of her phone call she praises both children again for playing so quietly and then gives Kayla a "high five" for playing so well. Then she suggests that Kayla give her friend a high five and she prompts Kayla to say to Jolie, "Good job Jolie." Kayla repeats this while giving her a high five.

Praise toddler's efforts

This mother helps the children understand the transition from her playing with them to their playing quietly for a few minutes while she is on the phone. She prepares both children by finding an activity that will interest them and keep them occupied. She keeps her telephone conversation brief, pausing to praise the children at a time when they are playing quietly and cooperatively. At the end of the phone call she again praises them for this quiet behavior. By suggesting her daughter praise her friend and by modeling the words for her, she is also teaching her daughter how to give compliments to others. This is a good example of the "shaping" we talked about earlier. She is beginning to shape their behavior to be quiet while she talks. She doesn't expect to have a 20-minute conversation at this stage but is praising them for the small steps needed to eventually be able to wait longer while she is on the phone.

Parents can help train their children to wait quietly during a phone call by praising their efforts to entertain themselves.

Self-Regulation

A major developmental milestone for preschoolers (three-five years) is to learn how to self-regulate and manage their anger and disappointment, but these skills emerge slowly, and are not fully developed until the early to mid-elementary school years. Toddlers (one-three years) are not yet ready neurologically or developmentally to utilize self-regulation skills such as waiting, taking turns, or staying calm when frustrated by something another child has done to them. Toddlers are easily frustrated because they can't easily communicate verbally what they feel or want, nor do they have the physical skills to do everything they want.

In the next scenario notice what behavior the mother is praising with her older child and think about what her toddler is learning from this praise to his sister.

Robin, a three-year-old, and his sister, Dorian, a six-year-old, are playing with blocks. Robin leans over to grab a block and accidentally knocks over his sister's structure. Dorian angrily tells Robin, "You knocked over my tower and broke it." She starts rebuilding her tower. Mother praises Dorian by saying, "Thank you Dorian for calming down and patiently putting it back together. That looked like an accident."

The mother in this scenario encourages Dorian's self-regulation and ability to manage her frustration. She focuses on her ability to calm down and rebuild the tower rather than on her angry words. If the roles were reversed, the mother would not expect Robin to be able to show this same level of self-regulation. However, if Robin repeatedly hears and sees his older sister using these skills while hearing his mother's praise, he will begin to learn these responses.

Thus although self-regulation is a key developmental milestone for preschoolers rather than toddlers, parents can still help their toddlers build the brain foundation for being ready to learn this skill. Parents can begin to help toddlers learn about self-regulation through the emotion coaching we talked about earlier and by combining this language with praise for times when they are calm, patient, or able to wait, even when something is frustrating. This approach helps toddlers link the peaceful feeling in their bodies with the verbal label. Moreover, you can help your toddler learn to self-regulate by modeling staying calm yourself and saying, "I'm getting frustrated, but I'm going to stay calm." You can also make an effort to understand what your child is trying to tell you, help provide her with the words or actions to address these needs or wants, and praise her efforts to communicate in a calm way.

Toddlers are easily frustrated because they can't easily communicate verbally.

Gentle Behavior

In the next scenario we see parents who are teaching their son, <u>Charlie,</u> how to be gentle with his cat. He has hurt the cat in the past with his aggressive patting. Notice how they praise and encourage the behavior they want to see more of.

Charlie is walking across the room with his cat, Simba, in his arms. His father asks him to be <u>gentle</u> and praises him: "I see you are holding her gently. She loves it when you do that." Later Charlie is lying on the couch with his cat and his father praises him by saying, "You are being very gentle and Simba is staying with you." Mother comments to her husband, "Simba looks happy, so Charlie must be doing a good job being gentle." Mother goes over to Charlie to check if he is being gentle and comments, "You are using nice, soft touch." Charlie replies, "I'm not being mean any more." Mother explains, "That means Simba likes to stay with you because you are being gentle." Charlie comments that when he is mean Simba has to run away from him. Mother praises him again for being gentle and tells him she understands this takes a lot of work. Charlie asks his mother to go away. He says, "I want to have fun with Simba alone." His mother replies, "Because you are being gentle, it is fair to let you have fun alone." She goes away and Charlie continues to be gentle with his cat. A little later mother comes back and says, "Look at that! Simba is still staying with you because you are being nice and gentle." She points out that Simba's eyes are closed and he is relaxing because Charlie is so gentle.

This mother is teaching her son what it means to be gentle. She does this by giving him labeled praise for his soft, gentle touches. She helps him understand the connection between his gentle touch and Simba's happiness and willingness to stay with him. She doesn't leave him alone long with the cat and continues to monitor and praise frequently the gentle behavior she wants to see more of.

Compliance

Remember it is normal for toddlers to resist or not comply with your requests. Toddlers are easily distracted, don't process verbal information in the same way adults do, and are driven to explore and be independent. This means that it is very important that you enthusiastically praise your toddler whenever she does listen or follow your request or the directions you give. This attention and praise will help strengthen your toddler's brain connections for compliance and cooperation with your instructions. At the same time, try to reduce the attention you give to your child's resistance or oppositional behavior. Instead, when you give directions such as, "Put on your shoes," "Use your spoon," "Sit in your car seat," "Wear your tricycle helmet," "Turn off the TV," be sure to praise compliance if your child does what you have asked. Don't take this compliance for granted! Through your praise and appreciation you will be teaching your child that doing what you ask is important and you value her efforts. With continued praise, you will find that your toddler will become less resistant and more helpful, although you can still expect her to exert her autonomy most of the time. And remember, if you ignore her helpful efforts, your toddler will soon learn to ignore your requests.

Be sure to praise compliance if your child does what you have asked.

Scaffolding Brain Development with Praise

We have been talking about the immense brain development and growth that occurs during the toddler years as new neuron connections are made. Parental coaching and praise can help strengthen links between positive social behaviors and the brain pathways for these behaviors. You can think of this as a scaffolding for learning that supports your toddler as you help her build the architecture of her emotional and social brain development. This social emotional brain development is just as important as the brain and muscle development that is needed to learn physical behaviors such as crawling, walking, and eventually running. In the next scenario notice how the father uses praise to scaffold his toddler as she learns to ride a tricycle. Think about what social and emotional skills and physical skills he is reinforcing.

> *A two-year old is outside on the sidewalk learning how to ride a tricycle. Her father helps place her feet where they should go on the pedals. He praises her when she does it correctly by saying, "Wow you have your feet exactly where they should go. You are really listening and trying hard." As she begins to pedal, he provides physical support and pushes the tricycle*

Parental coaching and praise can help strengthen links between positive social behaviors and the brain pathways for these behaviors.

a little to make it move forward. As the pedals move he comments enthusiastically, "See you are pushing hard with your feet. You are learning to ride." As his daughter struggles a little he comments, "That is a bit frustrating. You keep trying. You are doing it!" A little later he asks her to get off the tricycle so she can share it with her three-year-old cousin. He helps her get off and praises her enthusiastically by saying, "Wow you really listened and pushed hard and learned how to ride a tricycle. You worked hard and I really like the way you are sharing now with your cousin. That is so friendly. Let's watch together how she is peddling."

This father uses lots of scaffolding to encourage his daughter to learn how to ride a tricycle. He comments on the physical aspects of the task (placing her feet on the pedals, pushing hard, learning to ride) as well as the social emotional aspects (trying even though frustrated, listening, sharing, being friendly). It will be many years before she can actually ride a two-wheel bicycle independently and just as many years before she is able to be self-regulated, and exhibit social skills independently but he has begun the learning process in both areas. Her developing brain is laying down the neuron pathways for both social and physical competencies.

Praise scaffolding

Differential Attention – "Positive Opposite" Behaviors

Ignore the undesirable behavior you want to decrease while praising the desired behavior you want to encourage.

When thinking about behaviors you want to change with praise–think about the "positive opposite" of the behavior you don't want to see. So if your child is aggressive, praise her when she is calm or gentle. If your child is disobedient, praise her whenever she follows your directions. If your child is withdrawn and fearful, praise her when she is brave or tries something new. It is also helpful to combine praise with ignoring; that is, ignore the undesirable behavior you want to decrease while praising the desired behavior you want to encourage. This is called "differential attention." In the next scenario notice how the mother uses differential attention to promote the behaviors she wants to see more of. Notice what behaviors she ignores and what she praises.

A toddler is walking next to his mother, holding her hand and whining that he wants to go to the park. She does not respond to his whining, but instead says, "Billy, thank you for holding my hand. That's a good way to stay safe on the sidewalk." Then she points out a squirrel that is running in front of them. Billy stops whining briefly and says, "Squirrel running." Mother says, "Yes, that squirrel is running. I like the way you used your big boy voice to tell me that."

Proximal praise

Notice that instead of telling <u>Billy</u> to stop whining, his mother focused on the positive aspect of his behavior (holding hands). Next she used a distraction. When he responded, she was able to praise the positive opposite of whining (using a big boy voice). Thus Billy has learned that he gets more attention for the behaviors of holding hands and using a big boy voice than he does for whining.

Proximal praise is a variation on differential attention which is effective when you are with more than one child. When using proximal praise, you ignore a desired behavior in one child, while praising the positive opposite behavior in another child. Think about how this next mother does this:

<u>Robin</u> is licking his plate and his mother says, "Please use your spoon to eat." He ignores her and continues to lick his plate. Mother ignores this response by giving her attention to his sister, Dorian, and says, "<u>Dorian</u> thank you for using your spoon. You are using such polite manners at the table." A few minutes later she notices Robin using his spoon and enthusiastically praises him for this saying, "Robin, thank you for using your spoon. That's a lot of whipped cream that you are scooping up!"

In this scenario Robin got no attention for licking his bowl and Dorian was reinforced for using her spoon. Robin learned from this interaction and began to use his spoon. It is important that his mother then praised as soon as he started the positive behavior.

Doubling the Impact

Regardless of whether the reinforcer is attention, hug, smile, or verbal praise, the task of teaching a child a new behavior is a long and difficult one and often very slow. It means trying to praise that positive behavior whenever it occurs. If the behavior doesn't occur spontaneously, you want to prompt it, or model it so it does occur. If there are two adults in the family, both should talk about what behaviors they want to improve and what will be praised. In addition, adults can add to the impact of their praise by talking to each other about how well their child is doing, in front of the child. We saw this in a previous scenario when the father and mother talk to each other about what a good job Charlie is doing being gentle. They are doubling the impact of their praise by working together to encourage his gentle play with his cat. When one parent comments on a child's positive behavior to another parent it also serves to remind the other parent of the behaviors they are trying to encourage.

Combining Praise with Spontaneous Rewards or Celebrations

Coaching and praise will be the staple food for nurturing and supporting a toddler's social and emotional development. But every now and then you can give a surprise treat or reward to celebrate your toddler's success with learning something particularly difficult. These tangible rewards can include such things as a special fun sticker, a favorite food, a hand stamp, an additional privilege,

You can give a surprise treat or reward to celebrate your toddler's success with learning something particularly difficult.

an extra story time, or extra play time with a parent. These are given spontaneously for behaviors that are developmentally difficult for toddlers such as learning to use the potty, sharing a toy with a peer, putting on her shoes independently, getting dressed, staying seated at the dinner table, or sleeping all night in her own bed. Of course, these rewards are given with a heavy dose of parental enthusiasm and labeled praise to recognize the toddlers' achievement.

Building Up Your Own Praise and Support Bank Account

Praising, encouraging and coaching your children whenever they do something positive is the core of parenting. Moreover, your own ability to model effective communication, playfulness, empathy for another's feelings, anger management, praise and positive self-talk is also integral to the development of your children's social and moral development because children learn so much from watching and modeling your behaviors. However, no one is perfect and even the kindest and most well-intentioned parents get angry and frustrated with their toddlers. Parenting a toddler is challenging because of their need for constant attention and continual monitoring and supervision. At times, every parent gets exhausted, angry or stressed about all there is to manage with young children. You may be thinking to yourself, "She's driving me crazy, I can't stand it" or, "I've got so much household work to do, there is no time to play" or, "She wouldn't be so disobedient if I was a better parent" or, "I can't stand to hear that whiny voice for one more second." "She knows that this is wearing me down and she's going to keep it up till I snap." "She thinks this is funny and it's driving me nuts." Therefore it is important that you take the time to build up your personal bank account with deposits of love, support from others, self-care and self-praise and positive coping thoughts so that you can manage these difficult moments.

Personal Bank Account

Tips for Staying Calm

First remember all parents get stressed at times so use this feeling as a signal you need to take some time to refuel yourself physically and mentally. Don't let yourself catastrophize or exaggerate a problem or this will heighten your anger and outbursts. Instead stop negative and self-critical thinking and substitute more positive thoughts such as, *"I can control my anger, all parents feel like this at times, this feeling with pass," "I can stay calm and deal with this, all toddlers behave like this."*

Second, focus on some of your accomplishments. Think about a fun time you had playing with your child or something you did with your child that you are proud of. Go back and read some of your baby and toddler journal where you have written down some of the coaching and fun activities you did with your child. Praise yourself for all the work you have put into helping build your child's brain development by playing and coaching him. Remember to praise your own efforts and remind yourself of your long term goals.

Third, think about a possible positive solution to your situation (avoid blaming and focus on solutions) and what child behavior you want to target for further praise and coaching to help support your child.

Fourth, ask yourself when was the last time you rewarded yourself by taking a walk, having coffee with a friend, or exercised. Take some time out for yourself. When did you last praise yourself for your coping skills? Model your positive self-talk out loud for your children to hear at times. As your children observe these thinking responses, they will eventually learn to use them as well.

Stay calm, patient and relaxed

Fifth, reach out to another adult. Share your frustrations and then ask them to help you calm down, think of a solution to your problem, or distract you by talking about something unrelated to your toddler.

Sixth, try to find the humor in the situation. Although you don't want to let your child know that you are amused by her misbehavior, there just may be something just a little bit funny about her refusal to eat the peanut butter and jelly sandwich that you just cut into four pieces, at her request, and her wails to put the pieces back into a big sandwich. When she isn't looking, let yourself smile or save up the story to share with a partner or friend.

TODDLER ALERT

Remember to praise not only your child and yourself but also other family members or sitters and day-care providers who help you care for your toddler. This will not only build up your bank account with others but this modeling will be teaching your child the value of praising others in social relationships.

**Remember to Build Up Your Bank Account
with Other Family Members**

To Sum Up...
Reward Steps in the Right Direction

Remember behavior doesn't have to be perfect to warrant praise. In fact, when children are first learning a new behavior, they need praise and encouragement for each small step toward the goal. Without this encouragement they may give up altogether or resort to misbehavior to get some attention. This process of praising small steps in learning a behavior, known as "shaping," sets the child up for success. Effective praise and encouragement is labeled and specific, given with enthusiasm and warmth and combined with physical touch. You will find that when you put energy into praising, your child benefits and you feel good about yourself and your relationship with your child.

Praise and encouragement

Points to Remember about
PRAISING YOUR TODDLER

Every child is different. Spend some time observing your toddler and getting to know her temperament and reflect on the positive behaviors you want to encourage.

- Catch your child being good—don't save praise for perfect behavior.
- Don't worry about spoiling your children with praise.
- Increase praise for a difficult child by focusing on targeted "positive opposite behaviors.
- Model self-praise.
- Give labeled and specific praise for behavior you want to see more of.
- Make praise contingent on positive behavior.
- Praise with smiles, eye contact, and enthusiasm.
- Avoid combining praise with correction.
- Praise immediately.
- Give pats, hugs and kisses along with praise.
- Use praise consistently.
- Praise in front of other people.

**Remember to Build Up
Your Child's Bank Account**

Points to Remember

PRAISE AND ENCOURAGEMENT EXAMPLES

"You do a good job of…"

"You have learned to…"

"I like it when you…"

"Good for you for…"

"Good discovery of…"

"You've done a great job of…"

"See how _____ has improved in…"

"You're really trying hard to…"

"Look how friendly he/she was when…"

"That's an awesome way of…"

"Wow, what a careful job you've done of…"

"That's correct, that's a creative way to…"

"I'm so happy you…"

"It really pleases me when you…"

"You're such a big girl for…"

"Good boy for…"

"Thank you for…"

"What nice work…"

"Hey, you are really curious; you…"

"That's great, it really looks like…"

"You're doing just what Mommy wants you to do."

"My, you are minding Daddy so well."

"My! That…was so friendly."

"That's very kind…"

"Mommy's very proud of you for…"

"Beautiful! Fine! Great! Gorgeous! Tremendous!"

"How thoughtful of you to…"

Points to Remember about
STRENGTHENING PARENT SUPPORT– CARING DAYS

Partner Support

Conflict between partners can make it very difficult for parents to be effective in managing their children's behavior. The following exercise is designed to strengthen your relationship.

Identify 10 to 20 "caring" behaviors that your partner could do that you would enjoy. Ask your partner to do this also. List these behaviors on a piece of paper and post them. Each day you and your partner should try to select one or two items from the list and do them for one another. These caring behaviors should be (a) positive, (b) specific, (c) small, and (d) something that is not the subject of a recent conflict.

Examples: Ask how I spent the day and listen.
              Offer to get the cream or sugar for me.
              Listen to "mood music" when we set the clock radio to go to sleep.
              Hold my hand when we go for walks.
              Massage my back.
              Arrange for a babysitter and go out.
              Let me work late one night without a hassle.

Have a quiet dinner without the children.

Offer to watch the children while I make dinner, read the newspaper, etc.

Allow me to sleep in one morning on the weekend.

By doing this exercise, you will obtain a record of each other's efforts and become more observant of how the other person tries to please. We have noticed that parents are often quite willing to please their partner if they understand precisely what their partner wants and know that their efforts will be recognized.

Single Parent Support

If you do not have a partner, it is important to arrange some "caring days" for yourself. You could do this by developing a list of pleasurable things you would like to do for yourself. Each week pick at least one of the items from your list to give yourself.

Examples:　　Have dinner or go to a movie with a friend.

Exercise.

Arrange for a back rub or manicure.

Take a piano lesson.

Walk to the park.

Have a bubble bath.

Buy and read a fun magazine.

I take time for self-care and self-praise

It is also important for single parents to set up a support system. This might be done by meeting regularly with other parents, close friends, or family members. Organizations such as Parents Without Partners, church groups, recreational groups, and political groups can be sources of support and stimulation.

Parents' Viewpoint
MY TODDLER'S PRAISE JOURNAL

Write here the specific behaviors you are going to try to praise in your toddler. Then write down the exact praise statements.

Behaviors I want to see more of:	Praise statements I will use:

MY GOAL:

I will commit to increasing the number praises I give to my child to _____ per hour.

Parents' Viewpoint
POSITIVE SELF-PRAISE JOURNAL

For Parents

Write about a parenting moment or activity from the past week that makes you proud. This can be a fun parenting activity, a play time, or a moment when you responded effectively to your child.

Write down some of the positive self-praise thoughts that you will try to use to encourage your parenting efforts. Make a goal for yourself.

Example of Positive Self-Praise

I can do it…

I am working hard as a parent…

I can stay calm…

Remember to Build Up Your Own Personal Bank Account

MY GOAL:

I will commit to thinking about what I am doing well as a parent each day and give praise to others who are helping me care for my child.

POSITIVE OPPOSITES BEHAVIOR JOURNAL

Behaviors I want to see less of: e.g., hitting	For each negative behavior, put its positive opposite behavior below: e.g., staying calm and using words
1.	1.
2.	2.
3.	3.
4.	4.
5.	5.
6.	6.
7.	7.
8.	8.
9.	9.
10.	10.

11.	11.
12.	12.
13.	13.
14.	14.
15.	15.
16.	16.
17.	17.
18.	18.
19.	19.
20.	20.

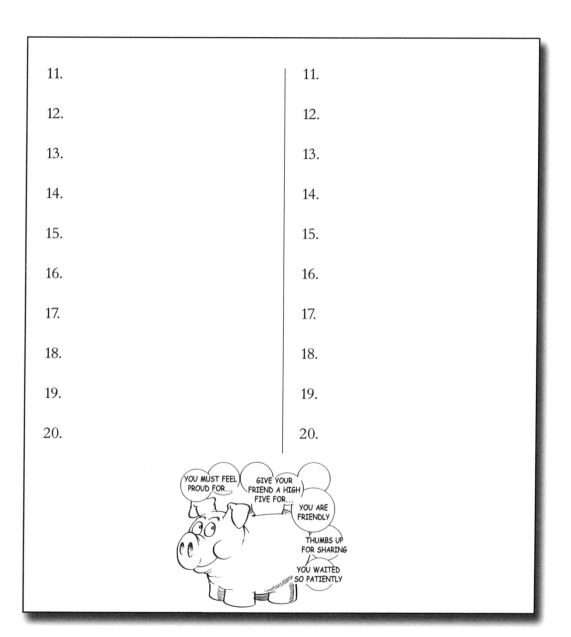

Parents' Viewpoint
MY REWARD JOURNAL

For Parents

Think about rewarding yourself. Have you ever used an incentive system to reward yourself for accomplishing difficult tasks or goals, like completing a difficult project, or working hard as a parent? Think about ways you could reward yourself for your hard work as a parent and record them below.

Things I Find Pleasurable and Rewarding:

Exercise or yoga class

Tea/coffee with a friend

Warm bubble bath

Buy myself a good book

I am developing a support team

MY GOAL:

I will commit to doing something positive for myself this week. This will include:

_____

_____

MY TODDLER'S PICTURE

CHAPTER 5

Separations, Reunions, Bedtime, and Routines

Introduction

In this chapter we move up to the fifth level of the parenting pyramid and will learn how to set up predictable schedules or routines for toddlers. Toddlers are creatures of habit and are often happiest when things stay the same! Although there is always variety in day-to-day life, your household routines will be important for helping your toddler feel safe and secure as well as loved. These routines can also help to prevent tantrums, misbehavior, and distress. Having routines, especially at times of the day when you need cooperation from your toddler or when there is a transition, will help both you and your child to get smoothly through the day.

Handling Separations

One important transition time is when you need to leave your toddler with another caregiver. In some households this happens when one parent leaves for work. In other households, the transition is drop-off at daycare, or the arrival of a nanny or other caregiver. Especially if the situation is new and unfamiliar, toddlers will usually show discomfort and be upset when their parent leaves them with a caregiver. This is a normal and healthy reaction and is a signal that your toddler is attached to you and will miss being with you.

You can help your toddler understand that you are leaving (and that you will come back) by setting up a predictable routine for saying good-bye each time you leave. Because toddlers now understand more language than previously and begin to realize that you are still around somewhere even if they can't see you, this explanation will help them feel safe and secure. It can be helpful to practice these separations and reunions at times when you are only leaving briefly, perhaps even to go into the other room for a few minutes.

In the next scenario, notice how this father responds to his 12-month-old baby, Patrick, when his mother leaves the room.

Mother leaves Patrick and goes to the kitchen to prepare some food and Patrick can't see her. Patrick cries out and father asks, "What is wrong?" Thinking that Patrick is upset about his mother's absence father reassures him by saying, "Mommy is right there. She is making some dinner." Patrick looks over to see if his mommy is there. He continues to be distressed because she is out of his line of vision. Father tells him, "Mommy will be back soon with some apple sauce."

In this scenario, the father does a great job of explaining to Patrick where Mommy has gone and reassuring him that she will be back. This helps Patrick understand what is happening. At first these explanations won't necessarily reduce his distress, but as he experiences this pattern enough times to believe that she really does come back, he will be more comfortable with the separation. Young babies do not have object permanence, which means that they can't remember you when you leave the room. This often means that they are relatively happy to be passed around to other caregivers. On the other hand, your toddler does understand object permanence and his distress when you leave means that he knows you are not with him and you are somewhere else and he wants you back where you belong! You can help your toddler prepare for your departure by telling him ahead of time that are you leaving. However, this does not guarantee that he won't show distress when you leave—that is a normal reaction.

In the above scenario the mother might say, "I am going to the kitchen to make dinner. I'll be back soon. You can stay with Daddy. Good bye Patrick." The predictable ritual you establish for leaving your toddler and saying "good-bye" is important to helping build your toddler's sense of security and predictability in his environment. These brief "practice" separations at home will help Patrick cope with longer separations in his daycare or with a babysitter.

Your toddler does understand object permanence and his distress when you leave means that he knows you are not with him and he wants you back.

Predictable routines

TODDLER ALERT

You may have noticed that your toddler is often distressed when one parent leaves, even if he is being left with another parent, a loved grandparent, or a well-known babysitter. This is very normal. At that moment, your toddler is more focused on the parent who is leaving than the parent or caregiver who is staying. If you are the parent who is staying behind, try not to take this personally: this distress is not a reflection of your relationship with your child. If you stay calm, give brief reassurance, and then distract your child with a game, toy, or change of venue, you will likely find that he will calm down and be happy with your company.

Play Peek-a-boo

Another way to help your toddler learn about object or person permanence is to play games like hide-and-find and peek-a-boo. In these games you hide, and your toddler finds you. This helps your child to know that even though you are not in his line of vision, you are still around somewhere. You can also play the game by putting a blanket over your toddler's face and saying, "Good-bye. Where has Patrick gone?" When he pulls the blanket off his face, say with excitement, "Hello, there is Patrick!" You can also do this with toys or stuffed animals. Toddlers will want to play this game over and over. They are enjoying the fun, but also working on understanding the predictability of separations and reunions.

They are enjoying the fun, but also working on understanding separations and reunions.

I teach person/object permanence

Separations and Reunions Routines

Having a constant ritual and routine way of leaving your child and returning at a regular time will help him to feel safe and secure in his relationship with you. Don't sneak away because you are afraid that your child will protest if you tell him you are leaving. This will only increase your child's insecurity about when you might unexpectedly disappear. Remember that distress is a normal reaction that will decrease as your child becomes used to the separation routine and the expectation of the predictable reunion. In the next scenario notice how these parents help prepare their two- and four-year-old children for the transition of the father leaving for work. Think about what makes their approach effective.

Mother explains, "We are going upstairs to say good-bye to Daddy who is going to work. After he goes, we are going to the supermarket." Four-year-old Daniel looks sad that his father is leaving. Father suggests, "Daniel can you be the captain and lead the way up the stairs? If you lead the way everyone will follow." Daniel keeps playing and ignores Father's request. Father starts to walk toward the stairs. Daniel gets up and says, " I will lead the way." Two-year old Lia is still playing with a car and Father announces, "Daniel is leading the way and I am going too." Mother repeats, "We are going to the supermarket and school after Daddy leaves." Mother picks Lia up and says, "Bye-bye car."

Did you notice that this mother calmly lets both children know that it is time to say good-bye to their father? She also lets them know what they will be doing next. This gives them time to mentally prepare for the separation and also the security of knowing what their next activity will be. The father's suggestion that Daniel be the leader is an effective way of easing this transition since it provides him with something fun to do and a sense of control. Although Daniel doesn't respond to this suggestion immediately, he does get up after a minute and then enjoys the game. Lia, the younger child, is less focused on her father leaving and more focused on the toy that she is playing with. Her mother helps her to make the separation from the toy by modeling that she can say goodbye to the toy and physically removing her. Using the same routine for leaving toys, places, and people will help toddlers learn that although they are saying good-bye, the separation is temporary. Both parents stay calm and avoid arguments or discussions about their children's reluctance to transition.

Regularity/ consistency of responses

Distress is a normal reaction that will decrease as your child becomes used to the separation routine.

Saying Bye-Bye

The same scenario continues and the father says good-bye to everyone in the family. Think about all the elements of this routine and why it is important for the children.

Daniel is looking unhappy. Father asks Lia for a good-bye hug and gives her a hug and kiss. He tells her, "I will see you this evening for dinner. Mommy will pick you up at school today." Lia accepts the hug willingly with very little distress. Next he says, "Daniel can I have a hug good-bye? I have to go to work now." Father hugs Daniel and says, "Thanks Daniel for being such a good bath taker and egg sharer this morning. Do you know who is picking you up after school today?" Daniel replies, " Mommy" and father agrees, "You are right and I will see you at home after that." He reminds him, "Tonight we will read some more of that Richard Scarry book." Father leaves and Mother says to Daniel, "It is a little sad when Daddy leaves, but we'll see him tonight." Lia says, "Bye-bye Daddy" and Daniel looks disappointed.

I say individual good-byes

This father takes the time to say individual good-byes to each of his children. These goodbyes are tailored to the children's ages and emotional responses. For Lia, who is younger and less distressed with the separation, he is affectionate and gives a brief message. For Daniel, who is older and more distressed, he adds a compliment about the egg sharing, a nice time that they had together during the morning.

This leaves him with a positive memory. He also reviews the reunion plans with both children, talking about who will pick them up from school at the end of the day and when he will see them next. Lastly, he talks with his son about a future positive event—sharing a story in the evening. After he says good-bye, the mother identifies Daniel's emotions, but reminds him about the reunion. The predictability of this routine each day will help these children to trust their parents and to feel safe.

TODDLER ALERT

It may be tempting to sneak out of the house when the baby-sitter arrives, or slip out of the daycare center when your child is not looking so that you can avoid a tearful parting. However, it is important to your child's sense of security that you say good-bye when you are leaving. In the short run, this is a harder thing to do, because most children will show distress at least some of the time. In the long run, however, this provides your child with a sense of security and control because he is confident and trusts that you will let him know when you are going and when you are coming back, and that you will follow through on those promises.

Greeting Children after an Absence

Try to leave your other worries or stresses behind when you see your child.

It is also important to have a predictable routine for greeting your child after you have been away for a while. When you return home from work, pick him up from day care, or even when he is waking up from a nap, be sure to show your joy and love at seeing him. Spending a few moments to reconnect will be important to re-establish your bond. The longer the separation, the more time your child is likely to need for this reconnection.

Sometimes this can be hard if you have had a stressful or difficult day at work or if you are rushing at the last minute to pick up your child from day care. If you seem stressed, annoyed, or unhappy when you greet your child after a separation from him, he may think your negative feelings have something to do with him and may feel anxious about his relationship with you. Therefore, be conscious of your initial greetings after a separation. Try to leave your other worries or stresses behind when you see your child. Try to make your greeting patient, relaxed, and joyful. This way the children will feel loved and wanted and will more easily reconnect with you.

Here are some key points for separating from and reuniting with children:

- Let your child know you are leaving; don't sneak away to avoid a tantrum, as this will increase your toddler's insecurity.
- Say good-bye briefly with a hug and say something positive about your expectations for their day.
- Let your child know when you will see him again and when he will be picked him up and by whom.

- Walk away and avoid giving too much attention to the child's normal protests.
- When you return, greet your child with love and joy—let him know you are happy to see him.
- Give him some transition time to separate from his current play experience.
- Understand that some children take longer to reunite than other children. If your child seems reluctant to reconnect with you right away, don't take this personally. Give him the space to adjust to the reunion by remaining nearby, staying positive, and allowing him to come to you when he is ready.

Joyful, patient and relaxed greetings

Bedtime Routine

Another important routine that needs to be consistent for young children occurs around the transition to going to bed and separating from parents at bedtime. When this routine is predictable, it helps children learn to settle to sleep and to feel secure. In the next scenario, notice the bedtime routine this parent has established for her three-year-old son, Robin, and think about what makes this effective.

Mother and Robin are picking out a bedtime story to read. He has picked two books and mother asks him, "Which book do you want to read first?" He chooses one and she says, "That is a good choice, I like that book too." They finish reading both books and mother says, "Time for bed now, sleep tight." She turns on Robin's music and says, "I love you, can I have a good night kiss?" He asks her, "Will I see you in the morning?" She reassures him, "Yes you will." He asks, "Can I sleep with you tonight?" She replies, "You can come down in the morning to my bed for a snuggle but you will stay in your own bed now. Nighty night." She kisses him again and gets up from his bed.

This mother does a nice job of setting up a predictable routine for bedtime. She reads to him in bed, which gives him time to make the transition and calm down from earlier activities. She reassures him of her love for him and that she will see him in the morning. She clearly sets the limit that he needs to sleep in his own bed and tells him she will reward him with a morning snuggle if he can do this.

Encouraging Children to Sleep in Their Own Beds

Now the scenario continues and you will learn how this mother continues her good-night routine with Robin. Think about the other strategies she is using to encourage him to fall asleep in his own bed.

Mother turns on music for him and says, "I will come back to check on you two times. Night night. I love you." She walks out. He replies, "I'm going to get all snuggled up." Later she comes back in and tells him, "This is one check." She gives him pat and says, "I will give you one more check." When she goes back for the second check he is asleep.

Telling children you will check on them is often reassuring to them.

The idea of telling children you will check on them is often reassuring to them. Usually by the time you do the second check they have fallen asleep. Some children have more difficulty falling asleep than others and the music can be a helpful distraction. This mother is "shaping" her child by rewarding his ability to stay quietly in his own bed each time she comes in to check on him.

Tips to helping your toddler develop healthy sleep habits

• Set a regular bedtime and regular nap times to regulate sleep patterns.
• Choose a bedtime that fits your family schedule and stick to it as much as possible.
• Establish a bedtime routine with quiet activities: calm play time, snack, bath time, pajamas, tooth brushing, story, song and kiss good night.
• If your child has trouble staying in bed, establish a checking schedule so that your child will be reassured that you will come back.
• Praise your child for staying in his own bed all night.

Picture Schedules

As toddlers approach three years of age, you can begin to use picture schedules to help them understand the steps of a routine. In the next scenario notice how this next father does this to help his three-year-old remember all the steps involved in getting ready for bed.

Father is explaining the bedtime routine to Robin, his three-year-old son. He shows him laminated pictures with magnets that are stuck to the refrigerator. Father explains, "This is something Mommy and I came up with to help you remember what you have to do at bedtime. These pictures are things that you do at bedtime." On one of the pictures the father draws a picture of his son in his pajamas. He asks him, "Does this look like you?" He colors in brown eyes and a big smile. Next he shows him other pictures of going to the potty, brushing teeth, and reading a story in bed. The father says, "When you do these jobs (potty, teeth, pajamas), then we will read a story in your bed!" The father asks him, "Which job will you do first?" Robins picks the picture of going to toilet. "Okay" says father, "You can go do that." Robin goes to the toilet and comes back in and father says, "Good job for going pee" and hugs him. Robin seems excited that he has done one of the things on the chart and moves the toilet picture magnet to a different part of the refrigerator to indicate he has done one of his nighttime jobs. Next they go off to brush his teeth. Afterwards the father praises his cooperation and thanks him and Robin moves that magnet card. When Robin has finished his three jobs (potty, teeth, pajamas) he seems excited and his father praises him enthusiastically and gives him a high five, "You did all your jobs so fast! Let's go read your book!" They go off to bed to read.

This father's routine is paced right at Robin's developmental level. There are only four simple steps in the routine, and the father has set up the sequence so that it ends with the most rewarding activity—the bedtime story. The pictures on the cards help Robin to "read" each of his jobs, which gives him a bit of independence with the system. His father involves Robin in the process of making the system by drawing the last picture while Robin is watching. He gives Robin some control by asking him which job he will do first. He is also available to provide scaffolding and support as Robin does each task. For the simpler tasks (going to the toilet) Robin goes alone, but he needs help brushing his teeth. At each step, Robin is given praise and encouragement. As this routine becomes easier for Robin, he will be able to have more and more independence, and eventually, the picture cards will not be needed because the tasks will have become second nature to Robin.

Young children have short attention spans and need help understanding and following any routine, especially if it involves more than one or two steps. The kind of picture chart used above with Robin can be useful for other routines such as getting ready for day care in the morning, or at dinner time or nap time.

Young children have short attention spans and need help understanding and following any routine.

Changes to Routines

Routines are particularly confusing for children if they vary from day to day so the more predictable you can make your routines, the faster your child will learn them. Moreover, predictability helps children to feel safe and secure. This does not mean that you must be a slave to your routine, and there are some benefits to children experiencing occasional changes in routines. If your child is supported through a change in a routine, it will help him learn to cope with changes and to be more flexible. Changes in routines will be easier for you and your child if you prepare for them.

If your child is supported through a change in a routine, it will help him learn to cope with changes.

Talk about the upcoming change and, perhaps think of a way to represent the change in a visual way. For example, if you will have a babysitter at bedtime, you might make a babysitter magnet picture. An hour before the babysitter arrives, you can have your child put the babysitter magnet on the chart and you can talk about this change and what it will mean. Since this change will also mean a separation, use some of the strategized outlines described earlier to support your child through the separation.

I talk about upcoming changes in routine

Determine Optimal Transition Lead Time

Remember that your toddler's experience of time passing is very different than your own, so make sure that you time your preparations so that your child has enough time to adjust to the change, but not so much time that he is needlessly anxious. For example, if you tell your three-year-old on Wednesday that he will have a babysitter on Friday, he will likely forget before Friday comes, or he may anxiously ask you every few minutes when the sitter

Time to process change

is coming. On the other hand, if you wait until 15 minutes before you leave to let your child know about the babysitter, he will not have enough time to adjust to the information and will likely have a harder time making the transition. It is also important to know that children are temperamentally different and vary in their ability to adjust to change and in their coping strategies. Experiment with your own child to determine his optimal lead-time for making a transition or for processing information about a change. Some children may benefit from a little more time while others will become anxious if they are told too far in advance.

TODDLER ALERT
When you leave your child with a sitter, it can be helpful to give a written list of your regular routine. The familiarity of the routine will be reassuring to your child even though you are not there.

Toilet Training Routines

 Sometime between the ages of two to five years old, most children begin to transition away from diapers and towards using the toilet independently. For many parents, this is an anxiously awaited milestone. The thought of not changing diapers anymore seems liberating, and often parents are faced with some time pressure from daycare centers or preschool programs that require children to be toilet trained. Remember that toilet training is a developmental milestone with huge variability! Try to approach this process with patience, humor, and the assurance that your child will not go to college in diapers, but that he will likely accomplish this goal at his own pace!

Many of the parenting principles we have talked about in this and earlier chapters can be used to help your child become toilet trained. Remember one of the most important ideas we have talked about is being "child-directed." This is particularly important in regard to toilet training. Remember that the toddler years are a time of increasing independence and wish for control. Also remember that having a bowel movement or urinating are two things that you can't actually make your child do. If

Child-directed toilet training

It is not uncommon for a four-year-old to still be working on all or some aspects of toilet training.

you show that this is something that is very important to you, your child may quickly learn that this is a place where he can exert a lot of power and control. This does not mean that you can't guide the process, only that you should do so with caution and a keen awareness of your child's viewpoint on the subject. First it is important to determine if your child is developmentally ready to be toilet trained. On average girls are toilet trained around 29 months and boys around 31 months. Remember that averages mean that many children will be trained earlier or much later than those ages. It is not uncommon for a four-year-old to still be working on all or some aspects of toilet training. Below are some signs that your child may be developmentally ready to start the toilet training process. Here are the first signs that your child is ready for toilet training to begin:

- your child can stay dry for three hours or more.
- your child recognizes the signs that he has to go.
- your child can pull his pants up and down by himself.
- your child seems interested or motivated in becoming potty trained.
- your child is imitating others going to the bathroom.
- your child can follow simple directions.

I practice patience when toilet training

If your child shows these signs of readiness you can begin the training process. Be sure to do it at a time when you have the patience and time and don't have too many other family pressures. Major transition times for your family or for your child (new daycare, new baby, new home) are not good times to begin toilet training and they may cause some relapses in preschoolers who already seemed to have been trained.

TODDLER ALERT:
Even if your child shows all the developmental signs of being ready to toilet train, he or she may resist your efforts to start toilet training. If this is the case, relax your efforts for a few weeks and then try again. Nothing will sabotage toilet training more than a power struggle between a reluctant child and an eager parent.

If your child seems ready, then you can set up a routine for sitting on the potty. Below are suggestions for a routine that may work. If you follow the guidelines of being child-directed, you may find a different routine that works better for you and your child.

1. Use a child-size "potty chair" or special adaptor seat for the toilet with a stool. When your child is sitting on the toilet, his feet should be able to rest comfortable on the floor or on a stool. You may want to involve your child in buying or decorating the potty chair and placing it in the bathroom.

Start by picking a regular time for a toilet-sit each day.

2. Invite your child into the bathroom when you or his siblings are going to the toilet and talk about what you are all doing. Suggest that sometime soon he will be big enough to use the potty all by himself. If he wants to sit on his potty (with or without his clothes), encourage him and praise him. Remember that children

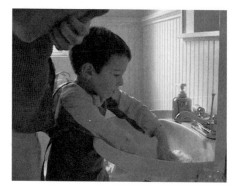

learn from your modeling. Show your child how you use the toilet paper, flush the toilet, and wash your hands.

3. To the extent that your child is interested, engage in pretend play with dolls or stuffed animals using the potty. Check out books and movies from the library that introduce the idea of toilet training.

4. Establish one predictable time each day that your child will try sitting on the toilet. If your child has a regular time for a bowel movement each day, this is a good time for the toilet-sit. If your child's bowel movements are not predictable, pick a time that will fit into your schedule in a relaxed way. If your child is willing and cooperative, you can have him sit naked on the potty. Otherwise, it is fine to have him sit on the

Routines and readiness

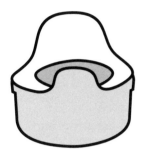

toilet fully clothed. See if your child will sit on the toilet for several minutes, perhaps while you read him a book. Don't worry if he doesn't have a bowel movement or urinate. Use your coaching and encouragement statements during this time so that he sees this as a fun event and don't force him to sit there. After three to five minutes (or shorter if your child is not willing), have him get up and praise him for sitting. If your child does urinate or have a bowel movement, praise his success.

5. Although your child is a long way from being independent in toileting this is a good time to change to clothes that will allow your child independence. Look for pants with elastic waists, and switch to pull-ups rather than diapers. Modern disposable diapers and pull-ups are so absorbent that children often do not feel the wetness when they urinate. You might consider switching to cloth pull-ups, at least for around the house, so that your child notices the wetness.

6. Once you have established a successful potty-sitting time once a day, you can switch to more frequent sits. Perhaps three times a day about two to three hours apart. When it is time for a potty sit, let your child know and let him help you check his diaper. If his diaper is dry, praise him and then have him sit. If his diaper is wet, still give praise for his cooperation with the check and say, "Maybe next time you'll be dry." You can still have him try sitting if he has a wet diaper. Again, remember not to require that your child is successful during the potty-sits. Praise cooperation with the process.

7. Let your child know that if he feels like he needs to go to the potty, he can ask for help. Give lots of praise for initiating on his own.

Remember not to require that your child is successful during the potty-sits. Praise cooperation with the process.

8. Expect that your child's interest in the process may wax and wane. Initially many children are interested in the novelty and will be enthusiastic. Then a few days or weeks later, they become indifferent or resistant. When this happens, give the process a break and begin again in a few weeks.

9. Even if your child is interested and motivated, expect accidents and setbacks. Don't make a big deal out of wet pants, wet beds, and other accidents. Stay calm and positive, "It's okay, next time I bet you will use the potty."

10. If your child is willing to sit on the potty, but has never had the experience of actually urinating in the toilet, you might want to consider having him spend some naked time in the yard (or in the kitchen). While this can be a messy proposition, it will help your child recognize the physical cues associate with urinating. You can point out when you see that he is starting to urinate so that he makes the connection. Try to do this calmly because if you startle him, you will make him tense up and will stop the urine flow. If he becomes aware of the feeling associated with urinating, he may be able to relax the necessary muscles when he is actually sitting on the toilet.

Even if your child is interested and motivated, expect accidents and setbacks.

I am patient and supportive

11. Once children have voluntary control over urination, toilet training becomes much easier because they are usually able to urinate soon after they sit down on the toilet. This is also a helpful stage for parents because now you will be able to suggest a toilet sit at strategic times (i.e., before a car ride, before and after naps, before a walk to the park). There is likely to be a stage in toilet training where your child can stay dry if you remind him to use the toilet every 2-3 hours. This stage often comes before children recognize the signs themselves, so if you forget the reminder, there is likely to be an accident.

12. Many children toilet train in stages. Some learn to have a bowel movement first, and then later learn to urinate. Others reverse this process and urinate first. Many children seem unwilling to have a bowel movement in the toilet and will ask for a diaper when they feel the urge. If you are patient and supportive with this process, it's likely your child will make the switch one day without much fuss or fanfare and won't look back. As with other stages of toilet training, if you push too hard, you may meet with more resistance.

13. Most children are toilet trained during the day long before they are dry at night. You might try limiting liquids two hours before dinner

> Once children have voluntary control over urination, toilet training becomes much easier.

Be calm and persevere

and making sure that your child urinates before going to sleep, but nighttime dryness is linked to developmental maturity and there is little that you can do to speed up the process. Children over the age of seven who are still wetting the bed at night might benefit from some other training methods, but during the toddler and preschool years, your best strategy is to keep your child in pull-ups until they are consistently dry at night.

Incentives for Toilet Training

Sticker charts will not generally be used until children are three years or older. However, sometimes a toddler can be given a spontaneous sticker or hand stamp for a special achievement. You might consider using a sticker chart or small reward to encourage your child to sit on the toilet (remember that you want to reward your child if he sits, don't require him to have a bowel movement or to urinate).

In the next scenario, watch how this mother praises her son for his bathroom routine.

Mother says to her three-year-old Ryan, "Okay remember after nap, what do we do?" Ryan replies, "Potty time." Mother responds, "You are right, you know exactly what to do, you are getting so big." He pulls down his trainer pants and sits on the toilet. When he finishes, he says, "I did it." His mother notices he has not gone to the bathroom but she replies, "Good for you! You get a sticker for pulling down your own pants and sitting on the toilet. She helps him pull up his pants and they put a sticker on his chart. She asks him what comes next?" He says, "Hand washing." She praises him again and lets him wash his hands himself. She puts the stickers away and gives him a big hug saying, "You remembered all three things, you are really learning. Now let's go and play."

The most important thing is that the process is fun.

The important thing here is that she is shaping all the routines and steps required for using the toilet. She does not require him to actually go to bathroom because at this point she is setting up her routine and praising him for remembering these things. She is remembering that he must be developmentally ready to use the toilet and is scaffolding his progress and readiness for this occur.

While the above example describes using stickers for rewards, you can use any small incentive that your child likes: a piece of special cereal, a gold fish cracker, a teddy graham, a hand stamp, an extra story, dancing to a song, a squirt of special lotion. The most important thing is that the process is fun and that you combine the incentive with your praise and encouragement.

Mealtime Routines

Just as with toilet training, using a toddler-led approach to eating is very important. Too often food fights occur and mealtimes become stressful because parents try to force their toddler to eat the food they have so lovingly prepared. In fact trying to make a toddler eat is a sure invitation to engage in a power struggle. Undoubtedly the spaghetti will end up on the floor. Save your energy for things that really matter. Remember it is your job to provide nutritious food and to decide where and how often you serve it, and it is your toddler's job to decide if he wants to eat it and how much gets into his mouth.

As we have seen toddlers like routine, and those routines carry over into the world of food. Your toddler may insist on having the same plate every day, or making sure the broccoli doesn't touch the mashed potatoes on his plate. No longer are they pushing food out of their mouth with their tongue to tell you they have had enough; now they are saying, "Yuck!" At 12-18 months they are still learning how to coordinate the muscles involved in chewing and swallowing and figuring out how

Your toddler may insist on having the same plate every day, or making sure the broccoli doesn't touch the mashed potatoes.

to steer their spoon into their mouth and will be highly distracted by texture, tastes and smells of food. They will be able to use a 'sippy' cup, enjoy eating with their hands and will love throwing food around to see how others react. At 18-24 months, they are getting more skilled with a spoon, developing food preferences, and are easily distracted while eating. At two to three years  they are becoming more skilled with their spoon but will still make a mess, have clear rituals about foods, may have food fixations and likely dawdle when eating. Despite their coordination difficulties all through toddlerhood their drive to be independent about feeding will be fierce.

At two to three years they are becoming more skilled with their spoon but will still make a mess.

Predictable routines can help make your mealtimes more enjoyable. For example, if your toddler is in the middle of building a really cool fort with his older brother in the living room and you ask him to come and eat, it will be pretty hard to settle at the table for his attention will be on returning to his fort. Instead, try to give plenty of transition time for your toddler to wind down from playtime and to get ready to

**Minimum
distractions
while eating**

come to dinner. Perhaps plan a quiet activity for the half-hour prior to dinnertime. Then allow adequate time for your toddler to eat so he doesn't feel rushed. It may not be that he is dawdling or is a picky eater but rather that he needs time to disengage from one activity and refocus on the next activity. During the meal keep distractions to a minimum and be sure to turn off the TV and telephone. On the other hand be sure to watch for warning cues that your toddler is restless and bored and is finished eating. When this happens lift her down from the high chair or booster seat. You can pair this with the words such as, "you may be excused," which will eventually lead to your preschooler being able to make this polite request. Remember it is not necessary for toddlers to sit for long periods of time at the table or to have a clean plate. If you have provided a relaxed mealtime atmosphere you can trust your toddler to eat the right amount of food. You will notice your toddler will eat more at some meals than others as they are naturally adjusting their food intake according to their energy needs.

It is not necessary for toddlers to sit for long periods of time at the table or to have a clean plate.

Tips for making your mealtimes enjoyable as well as allowing your toddlers to have some independence:

- Offer a variety of different types of simple foods so your toddler has choices.
- Make foods appealing by providing different colors, shapes, textures; you could even cut your grilled cheese sandwich into animal shapes with cookie cutters.

- Offer foods at room temperature that are soft and easy to chew.
- Stick to toddler size portions of food and avoid too much food; allow him to come back for seconds if he wants.

- Offer only one new food at a time and pair it with a food the toddler likes; avoid any pressure on your toddler to try the new food; model eating it yourself.
- Involve your child in aspects of food preparation such as participating in grocery shopping, growing an herb garden, to washing carrots or lettuce.
- Don't get into battles over food – like toilet training this is a battle you can't win.
- Respect your toddler's preferences for particular foods but don't let it dictate your family menu.
- Allow your toddler to help by putting napkins on the table or sponging after a meal or putting things in the garbage.
- As your toddler approaches three years of age, you may be able to engage him in a game of "thumbs up or down." Encourage him to try a new food and let you know with his thumb whether he likes it.

 TODDLER ALERT
Make sure toddlers under 18 months don't have a daily juice intake exceeding 4 ounces or for those over 18 months the 8 ounce maximum. Dilute the juice with water.

Toddlers have fairly high energy needs and small stomachs, so most will need to eat every two to three hours. Therefore, plan in your routine to offer your toddler a healthy snack midway between breakfast and lunch, and between lunch and dinner and at bedtime. These snacks should be packed with nutrients such as whole-grain crackers or rice cakes, dry cereal (Cheerios) with finely chopped dried fruit, oatmeal cookies (made with whole wheat flour), sliced finger-size fruits and vegetables with yogurt for dipping. Limit sugary foods to prevent tooth decay and avoid sweetened or non-pasteurized fruit juice drinks or punches.

TODDLER ALERT

It is normal for toddlers to refuse new foods and it takes time for toddlers to like them. Studies have shown that toddlers have to be exposed to a new food on as many as 15 different occasions before they will actually eat it!

Toddlers often develop a fixation on a particular food and want to eat it at every meal. Fish sticks and Kraft Macaroni and Cheese were my children's favorites. Fortunately these food jags tend to be temporary and it is usually better to go along with it rather than trying to fight it.

TODDLER ALERT

If you offer plenty of healthy options, from all the food groups and limit unhealthy options, most toddlers will eat a balanced diet, across several days. So, your toddler may eat only fruit at one meal, and only cheese at another, or will only eat cereal and bread for a whole day. However averaged together these choices will balance out and provide the nutrients your child needs. This will not be true if you offer high sugar foods or other junk foods.

Reading Routines

You can read at any time but make sure it is a time when you are relaxed and attentive.

Developing a daily reading routine is a good idea because it can become a habit for you and your child for years to come. This is a time when your toddler has your undivided attention and will not only contribute to your toddler's language development but also continue to foster a close bond between you. You can read at any time but make sure it is a time when you are relaxed and attentive. For

specific tips for making reading fun, reread pages 92-95 in chapter 2. Here are a few tips to promote your toddler's regular reading enjoyment and independence:

Age 12-18 months

Of the 50 or more words that your toddler can now say, many of those will have come from the many books you have read frequently.

- Allow your toddler to select the book he wants to read from his favorites.
- Allow your toddler to stand, lie down, or sit while you read. Allow him to be in control of turning the pages at will and choosing the pages you read.
- Continue parent-ese interaction and use sound effects for animals, vehicles and actions.
- Re-read favorite books and stories and dramatize the sequence.
- If you start reading and your toddler squirms off your lap that doesn't mean he wants to stop reading. Ham up the story and see if he stops to listen.

Remember it is normal for toddlers to be very active and have a short attention span. When they are tired and less active can be a good time to read.

18-24 months
Although the amount of spoken words varies, at this time your toddler will understand most of your conversations.

- Encourage talk through some open-ended questions.
- If your child mispronounces a word, just repeat what your child said, but say the sounds correctly and let it go at that.
- Slide your finger under the words on the page to show your toddler that the letters have meaning.
- Encourage older siblings to read with your toddler.

I have a daily reading routine

To Sum Up...

The toddler age and developmental milestones include the vacillation between dependence and independence. One minute toddlers want to be independent and do it themselves and the next they need the security and support of a parent. They are learning to trust their environment and to develop intimate attachments with their parents and caregivers. All your toddler-directed coaching and praise will help them develop a sense of their own individuality and who they are as persons. But predictable routines and schedules regarding separations and reunions, bedtimes, meals, toilet training and reading times are very important for helping them to feel secure and safe and for reducing tantrums, anxiety and stress.

Points to Remember about
HANDLING SEPARATIONS AND REUNIONS

Most children will have mastered separation anxiety by three years; but temporary episodes of separation anxiety are normal. Toddlers vacillate between wanting to be independent and needing the security of a parent. Especially if your toddler is shy or timid, you will find that helping your toddler cope with separations will result in a more secure and confident preschooler. But don't worry, there are still many years left before independence is fully achieved.

I say brief good-byes

- Let your child know you are leaving in a predictable, routine way–don't sneak away to avoid a tantrum or lie about where you are going, as this will only increase your toddler's insecurity.
- Say good-bye briefly with a hug and say something positive about your expectations for your child's time away from you. Reassure him in a positive way that he will have a good time when you are gone and that he's safe.
- Encourage your child's growing independence.
- If you are leaving your child at day care, let him know when you will see him again and when he will be picked him up and by whom.
- If you are leaving him at home and going out for the evening, let him know who will be taking care of him and when you will be back. For example, "Grandma is coming to play with you tonight while I go out for dinner. I'll be home after you are in bed, but I'll come in and kiss you good night."
- Leave and avoid giving too much attention to the child's normal protests.

- When you return greet your child with love and joy–let him know you are happy to see him.
- Give your child some transition time to move from his current play experience to leaving with you.

Happy greetings

Points to Remember about
PICKY EATING

Eating solids is a new learning experience for your toddler. Your child will need time to explore the tastes, textures and smell of each new food. Remember repeated learning trials will be needed before your toddler will come to like a new food.

I provide some food choices and independent decision-making

- Try to make mealtimes a regular, relaxed, time limited and fun time for your toddler.
- Minimize distractions during mealtimes by turning off TV or taking the phone off the hook.
- Provide your toddler with a choice of foods to allow for independent decision making.
- Introduce one new food at a time in a small amount; for example, offer the new food along with your toddler's favorites.
- Try to offer a meal with at least one food choice you know your toddler likes.
- Offer toddler-size portions–which are much smaller than adult portions.
- Resist the urge to offer sugary foods, or your toddler will learn to prefer these foods over others.
- Don't expect your toddler to like a whole lot of foods–let your toddler make his own decisions on the food he chooses to eat. Forcing your child to eat will only make your toddler more stubborn and less open to new foods in the future.
- You don't need to become a short-order cook. If you provide some choices of foods your toddler often likes, you don't need to cook an entire new dinner to meet his demands.

Points to Remember about
TOILET TRAINING READINESS

Most children are trained by three years but don't worry if your 3-year-old isn't trained; some children aren't ready until they are four years old. If your child shows signs of readiness you can begin toilet training about 2½ years. Avoid rushing or getting into power struggles over this. Do this training when you have the time and patience and don't have too many other family pressures.

Signs of Readiness
- your child can stay dry for 3 hours or more
- your child recognizes the signs that she has to go
- your child can pull down her pants down and up by herself
- your child seems interested or motivated to become potty trained
- your child is imitating others going to the bathroom
- your child can follow simple instructions

Avoid power struggles

Points to Remember about
STARTING TOILET TRAINING

I expect accidents

- Dress your child in clothes that are easy to get undone such as elastic-wasted pants.
- Use a child-sized potty chair or special adaptor seat with a stool.
- Create a routine for sitting on potty–start by seating your child fully clothed once day, whenever s/he is most likely to have a bowel movement.
- Progress to sitting your child on the potty bare-bottomed. Don't restrain or force your child to sit there.
- Let your child watch you or older sibling go to the bathroom.
- Show your toddler how you use the toilet paper, flush the toilet and wash your hands.
- Praise your child every time she uses the potty seat, or you check and she has dry pants.
- Set up a schedule for going to the bathroom.
- Make sure your child knows it's okay to ask for help to go to the potty anytime.
- Teach your child how to clean and wash hands after going to the potty.
- Expect set backs; don't make a big deal out of mistakes such as wet beds or accidents–stay calm and positive, "it's okay, next time I bet you will use the potty chair."

- Once training is established, consider using training pants as this allows a toddler to undress by himself; introduce them gradually maybe for a few hours at a time.
- Keep using diapers at night; even though your toddler is dry during the day, it can take months or years before children are dry at night.

Praise your child

MY TODDLER'S READING JOURNAL

Keep track of the names of your toddler's favorite books and stories. Add a photo to this page of your toddler and you reading.

OUR SEPARATION ROUTINE

Write out your routine for leaving your child at daycare.

OUR FAMILY BEDTIME ROUTINE

Write out your bedtime routine here.

OUR FAMILY MORNING ROUTINE

Write out your morning routine here.

OUR TOILET ROUTINE

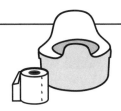

Write out your toilet routine here.

MY TODDLER'S PICTURE

Take a picture or your child following a routine here.

CHAPTER 6

Positive Discipline and Effective Limit Setting

Introduction

So far we have been moving up the parenting toddler pyramid discussed in chapter one, from child-directed play, various coaching methods and praise, to routines. You have probably already found that when you have built a solid foundation of parental attention to positive behavior and regular, predictable routines, things go more smoothly. This is because you have invested in your children and they know what to expect in your day to day activities. In this chapter we will discuss ways to use positive discipline methods such as distractions, redirections, ignoring and clear limit setting and how to follow through and cope with toddlers' inevitable protests. If you have built up your positive attachment bank account, you will have something to draw from when using discipline and your children will want to return to their positive relationship with you.

Most toddlers fail to comply with parents' verbal requests the majority of the time.

Did you know that part of the definition of discipline means to "teach"? So through your coaching, prompting, modeling, praising, respectful responses, and predictable routines you have already been engaged in the process of disciplining, scaffolding and strengthening your child's appropriate social, emotional, and cognitive brain connections and pruning the inappropriate ones. However, remember that it is part of a toddler's job to test limits, so tantrums, pushing, biting, and saying "no" will most likely be frequent occurrences. Research shows that most toddlers fail to comply with parents' verbal requests the majority of the time. You will by now understand why it is not helpful to yell, hit, slap, or lecture your toddler as these methods model disrespectful behavior and strengthen the very neuron connections you don't want to encourage. Ultimately these negative parent responses will result in more misbehavior from your child—even if at first these approaches may seem stop your child's behavior in the short run.

The first step in managing your toddler's misbehavior is to recognize that toddlers are not deliberately misbehaving but actually are biologically programmed to explore, to touch things, to be curious, to be aggressive, and to test the limits as part of their normal development drive. They are moving from the stage of being passive and dependent as babies to the exploration stage which is thought to help children develop a sense of autonomy, independence, sense of self, and eventually self-control. Moreover, toddler's limited language ability means they often don't understand verbal requests or directions nor are they able to express their needs verbally to others. Therefore you can actually expect them to resort to more physical and negative behaviors and protests to get what they want or when they don't understand what is happening or can't express their desires.

It is a challenging task for parents to allow toddlers some freedom to discover while at the same time keeping them safe by supervising and monitoring them closely. Parents must find ways of establishing clear and necessary limits when needed and teaching appropriate social skills while avoiding giving too many unnecessary directions, getting angry, or saying no too often. On the following pages, you will find some of the problems parents frequently encounter when setting limits with their toddlers and some effective ways to give directions or commands and set limits.

TODDLER ALERT

Be sure to recheck your Toddler-Proofing Checklist in chapter one to make sure you have removed all dangerous items.

Avoid Unnecessary Commands

The average parent gives almost one command or correction every minute. This means that in an hour of parent-child time, children are told to do or stop doing about 60 things! Imagine if your boss or spouse expected you to follow that many commands. Do you think you would be willing or even able to cooperate? If you put yourself in your child's shoes, you may start to see why an excessive number of commands may actually lead to more noncompliance and negativity from your child. Several things happen when parents give frequent commands. First, children are usually unable or unwilling to follow that many commands either because they are overwhelmed or angry or have learned to tune them out. Parents may respond to this noncompliance by repeating the command (perhaps with increasing irritation) or dropping the command (and letting the child get away with non-compliance). In the first instance, the parent's repeated command gives negative attention to noncompliance, reinforcing the noncompliance. In

Too many "no's" or limits will conflict with your toddler's drive to explore and cause you both frustration.

the second instance, children receive a mixed message–sometimes the parents really mean it when they give a command, and at other times they don't seem to care whether the children comply. In both instances, the parent's intention that the child do what is asked is undermined and the net result is more non-compliance and frustration from both parties. One of the first steps in giving effective commands is to eliminate unnecessary commands so that you can focus your efforts on the really important ones. Too many "no's" or limits will conflict with the toddler's drive to explore and cause you both frustration. In the next scenario see if you think these commands are necessary and whether you might respond differently.

A mother and her two children are having lunch. Mother says to her daughter, "You need to try some cottage cheese, it's right there. Scoop up some cottage cheese." And then she says to her son, "Dion, I want you to eat all of that cottage cheese." Dion eats some cottage cheese and his sister begins to serve herself some cottage cheese. Mother responds, "Eat salad Denise" and Denise says, "I don't like salad." Mother insists, "Well, I know, but today you're going to eat your salad, Denise." Denise continues to put cottage cheese on her plate. Mother says, "OK, that's enough cottage cheese. Now put the lid on." She turns to Dion saying, "Stop using your fingers to eat."

In that brief interaction this mother gives eight separate commands. Her goal is to get her children to eat a healthy meal, but she has fallen into several traps that will undermine her attempts. Her commands are given rapid-fire without sufficient time for compliance. This may make it difficult for her children to even process the many things she is asking them to do. It is likely that they don't hear all her commands. However, both of her children do try to comply with one of her requests and start eating some cottage cheese. At this point she fails to praise this cooperation which makes it very unlikely they will continue the behavior. Overall this mother is giving

I avoid mixed messages

more attention to her children for what they are not eating which inadvertently reinforces their reluctant eating habits. By ignoring the behavior she wants to encourage (eating cottage cheese), this mother is teaching her children that they will receive more attention from her for not eating than for eating. Few parents are aware of the actual number of commands they give their children. Therefore, one of the first steps to giving more effective commands is to evaluate the type and number of commands that you are currently giving and to try only to give commands that are necessary.

Limit number of commands

Necessary Commands

Every parent will have different ideas about which commands are important and necessary. Typically for toddlers, important commands will be those that involve safety such as riding their tricycle in a safe place, wearing a seat belt or bike helmet, taking a parent's hand when crossing the street, or keeping their hands to their own body. Another category of commands that are likely to be necessary are those that involve getting a child out of the house at a designated time so that a parent can go to work or commands associated with regular important routines like bedtime or naptime. One rule of thumb is that you should not give a command that you are not prepared to follow through on, so before you speak, think about whether the command is worth a battle if your child doesn't comply. This may lead you to decide that commands about what a child will wear, what and how they build a block tower, how many bites of supper they eat, or how they color a picture are better left unsaid.

You should not give a command that you are not prepared to follow through on.

Once you have reduced your unnecessary commands to the important ones, then your children will learn that they are important and their compliance is expected. You may also be surprised that even when you have reduced your commands to those that are necessary, there are still many things that you ask your toddler to do throughout the day. When you remember that a toddler's main developmental task is to achieve control and independence, you can see why they are often in conflict with their parents!

TODDLER ALERT

Reduce your commands to the most important ones that you are prepared to follow through on. You should have at least 10 more positive coaching and praise statements than commands or corrections.

Remember Predictable Routines

I am consistent and predictable

In chapter 5 we talked about the importance of establishing clear and predictable routines for saying goodbye to your children at day care or with baby-sitters, when going to bed, taking a bath, getting dressed in the morning, or ending a fun activity. This consistency will not only help your children to feel safe and secure in their relationship with you, but will reduce the number of commands you need to give because your children will learn the routine and know exactly what happens next without needing to be told each step. In other words, the predictability of the routine will eventually lead to an increase in compliant behavior. Be patient with this process, because children will need to experience and practice each routine many times before it becomes habit.

Distractions and Redirects

One of the most effective strategies for getting toddlers to do what you want, or to stop them doing something, is to offer them an interesting distraction and redirect their attention. For example, removing the remote control from a toddler's hand while offering her an acceptable plaything may avert a meltdown. Here, the idea is to shift her focus from what she can't do to what she can do. Thus the parent encourages autonomy while setting a limit on inappropriate behavior.

Since toddlers frequently want to play with or touch things that are dangerous or inappropriate, it is a good idea to have a ready supply of safe, acceptable play things that you can quickly pull out as a distraction. For instance you may have a kitchen drawer of pots, pans, wooden spoons, utensils that are not dangerous that are available for your child to play with. If she is demanding the knife you are using to prepare dinner you can say, "This knife is dangerous, let's see if we can find something in your drawer for you to use."

In the living room you might also have a box of special toys. In this way if your toddler wants to touch something that shouldn't be touched (such as DVD player) you can offer a substitute and redirect your child's attention to the toys to play with. For example, you might say, "You can't jump on the couch but you can get your Duplos out."

> It is a good idea to have a ready supply of safe, acceptable play things that you can quickly pull out as a distraction.

Giving Choices When Possible

For toddlers who are searching for autonomy, it can be helpful when possible to limit set by giving them a choice. Commands that prohibit your child from doing something should include suggestions for what they can do instead. You might say, "You cannot watch TV now, but you can play with this play dough with me." Such an approach can help reduce power struggles because, instead of fighting about what your child cannot do, you're refocusing your child on some other positive activity. In the next scenario a father is helping his toddler, Lia, take a bath. Notice how he sets a clear limit as well as how he allows his daughter a choice when giving the instructions.

Lia wants to turn the bath water on and Father says, "We don't need the water on, do you want to use the washcloth yourself or for me to do it?" She chooses to use the wash cloth herself and he says, "Wow you really know how to wash your face yourself!" Later he asks, "Do you want to put the shampoo on or do you want me to do it?" Again she says she wants to do it herself so he puts the shampoo in her hand and says, "Rub your hands together." As she puts the shampoo on her head he says, "Perfect you really know how to shampoo your hair, you are getting so big."

Instead of giving a command, this father offered two choices. By asking if she would do it herself or if he would do it, she was allowed some control over the situations and could choose an option that allowed her to be more independent. As a result she complied with his requests. Indeed giving a young child a choice will often prevent a power struggle from occurring and give the child a chance to appropriately exercise their control. Remember, however, that you want to structure the choices such that either choice is acceptable to you. Notice the difference between these two choices "Do you want to go to the potty before or after I do?" versus "Do you want to go to the potty now?" If you really want your child to try the potty, then the second option is not a good way to phrase the choice. Also remember that young children can be overwhelmed by too much choice, so limited options may be more effective than open ended ones. For example, "Do you want to wear the red shirt or the blue shirt?" rather than "What shirt do you want to wear?"

Young children can be overwhelmed by too much choice, so limited options may be more effective .

Offer limited choices

When-Then Commands or Requests

Sometimes it is not possible to give a child a choice. When this is the case, it can be very effective to use a "first-then" or "when-then" command or request—that is, letting your child know what positive event will happen after they have finished doing what you want them to do first. For example, "When you finish getting your shoes on, then you can play with the doggie" or, "When you pick up your toys, then we will get your favorite snack." First you get the appropriate behavior you want and then you provide some positive consequence. This strategy allows the toddler to anticipate the positive outcome of following her parents' request; making it more likely she will cooperate.

In the next scenario we see Lia's four-year-old brother playing in the bath. Think about the father's use of when-then commands and see if you can identify the strategies he uses to help Daniel accept the limits.

Four-year-old Daniel is taking a bath and his father asks him to wash his body. Daniel resists, "I want to keep playing with the boat." Father picks up the toy boat and puts it next to the bath tub saying, "When you've washed your body, then you can play for 5 more minutes." Daniel starts to whine, but Dad hands him the wash cloth saying, "Let's see how fast you can get clean!" Daniel begins to wash and Dad says, "Wow! You are getting so clean. You'll be able to play again very soon!"

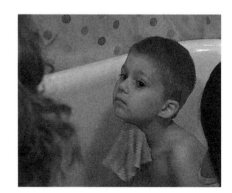

In this scenario the father gives Daniel a "when-then" command. The command is effective because the "then" is something that he knows that Daniel wants to do. He also sets up the command effectively by removing the toy boat as he gives the command, so that Daniel will need to comply in order to get the boat back. This father enhances the effectiveness of his when-then statement by pairing it with a challenge to see how fast Daniel can wash, and by praising his first efforts to do so.

TODDLER ALERT

A when-then command should only be used in an instance where you are willing to let the command go if the child doesn't comply. For instance, if Daniel, had decided not to wash, the father's recourse would be to say, "Okay, that's your choice, but I'm going to put the boat away and it's time for you to get out of the bath." In cases where you must have your child comply, a when-then command is not the best strategy to use.

Use Polite, Clear, Short and "Do" Commands

It is not always feasible to give a toddler a choice or to use a when-then command. Sometimes a clear command is the best option, especially when a child's safety is involved. Keep your commands clear, short and to the point. It also helps to have eye contact with your child. Try not to give commands with too many words or explanations. Verbose commands will likely be confusing to the child and distract her from hearing what behavior is expected of her. Here is example of the father we talked about earlier limit setting with Lia at breakfast time when he notices she is standing up precariously in her high chair.

Father says politely, "Please sit down. Tush on seat." He goes over to her and repeats the instruction, "Please sit down" and pats her high chair seat saying, "Tush on the seat please." She sits down and he responds, "Thank you. Good sitting. You are a good girl." She asks, "Why" and he explains, "You might fall, and you won't be safe." Next he distracts her by asking, "Are you ready for some yummy yogurt?"

My commands are clear and positive

Avoid criticism

This father's request is clear, positive and focused on the positive behavior he wants from Lia. An alternative response might have been to say, "Stop standing on your chair" but this would have defeated his purpose because he would be describing the negative behavior rather than the positive behavior he wants to occur. He keeps his request simple—three words at a time—so as not to overwhelm or confuse her with too much language. Also he does not rely on her understanding the words in this instruction, but goes over to her, signaling nonverbally with a pat on her high chair to show where she needs to sit down. His follow through and attention for her compliance was immediate, positive and clear. He avoids an argument about this by distracting her attention to what she will eat next.

Avoid criticizing your toddler when you make a request or getting angry about misbehavior. You might be frustrated because you have likely told your toddler the same thing many times before, however the feeling expressed behind the request is just as important as the actual words being used. If your child senses your anger, she may feel incompetent, defensive, and less inclined to comply as a way of retaliating for your anger. Requests should be delivered simply, clearly and politely with the action verb of the behavior you want to see at the beginning of the request, "Walk slowly," "Gentle touch," "Hands to body," "Quiet voice." If the positive desired behavior is given first in your instruction, it will be more likely your child will hear it.

Avoid criticizing your toddler when you make a request or getting angry about misbehavior.

Actions Speak Louder than Words

Sometimes in order to keep toddlers safe the instruction or command needs to be followed through with immediate parental physical action. For example, your toddler is riding her tricycle on street rather than on the sidewalk, you remind her of the rule, "Ride your tricycle on the sidewalk. The street is not safe" and right away you go over and move your child to the sidewalk. In other words you don't rely on your toddler to understand your verbal request, but you combine your verbal with physically moving your child to the correct place. Whenever you see your toddler in a potentially unsafe situation, you want to give a command focusing on the positive alternative behavior you want to teach coupled with your behavioral action so there is immediate follow through. Another example would be asking your toddler to turn off the TV. You give a polite command with a positive consequence for complying, "Turn off the TV, Anna, and let's bake cookies together." However, most toddlers will not comply and are too enticed by the immediacy of the TV to have the self-control to turn it off. You will need to combine your request with the action of going over to your child and helping her turn off the TV. You might say, "Do you want to turn it off by yourself, or should I do it?" Thus you are still giving the child an opportunity or choice to do this independently but you are assuring your request will be followed.

In the examples above all these parents were limit setting without saying "no." Children under age three have difficulty with the concept of "no" because it is in direct opposition to their developmental drive or job to explore and assert self-control. Therefore, if you say "no" to your toddler, don't expect she will stop every time or right

If you say "no" to your toddler, don't expect she will stop every time or right away.

away. Try to avoid getting angry when she doesn't stop, for your attention could reinforce the oppositional behavior. Keep your "no" as calm as possible and avoid nagging "no's" or too many "no's." Instead, use the "no" as a cue there is a limit being set and after you say no, give your positive command, redirect, distract or physically move your toddler to something else. When your toddler does stop when you ask her or tell her "no," be sure to give her lots of praise for listening. Because toddlers have such a drive to test and explore, supervision of them at all times is crucial so that parents can keep them safe.

Logical Consequences

I create age-appropriate consequences

Most logical and natural consequences work best for children four years and older who have the cognitive skills to understand the relationship between the consequence and the misbehavior. They can be used once in a while with toddlers, but parents must first evaluate carefully whether their expectations are appropriate for their age. For example, letting a toddler or a preschooler experience the natural consequence of sticking a finger into an electric outlet, or touching the stove, or running on the road would be unsafe and developmentally inappropriate. Occasionally parents come up with consequences that are not logically related to the misbehavior. Consider the mother who washed her son's mouth out with soap because he said something bad. While she might argue that it is logical to clean out the mouth of a toddler who has been swearing, this is more likely to make her son feel dirty and degraded. Other parents create consequences that are too punitive. For example, "Since you bit your friend, I'm going to bite you." Children will feel resentful, angry and perhaps even retaliate against such consequences. They will be more focused on the cruelty of the parents than on changing their behavior. In the next example, think about how the parent uses a logical consequence effectively for her 18-month-old toddler.

Make the consequence immediate, short, to the point and then quickly offer your child a chance to try again.

Mother notices Lia has a sharp knife in her hand. She says assertively, "I am going to take that knife away from you, it is not safe" as she is removing the knife from her daughter's hand. (immediate action and logical consequence) Lia protests and mother remains calm and hands her a wooden utensil, "Here's something safe you can cut with."

Here the age-appropriate consequence involves immediately protecting the child from the possible negative outcomes of her behavior. The mother avoids too much talking and distracts her daughter to another similar activity, which is safe. At two to three years, when children can understand the connection between their behavior and the outcome they can be used as long as they are immediate, and stated in a calm, matter-of-fact, friendly voice. For example, saying, "If you don't help to clean up the toys, then I will put them away until after nap. Or, "If you can't sit in the chair on your bottom, you will need to  get down from the table." Or, "If you throw a block at the window, I will put it away." It is important to be straightforward and assertive about consequences and be prepared to follow through with them, and to ignore your child's protests or pleading. Remember your child will test the limits, so expect it. Once the toy has been removed give them a new opportunity to be successful. For example, three-year-old Seth is using crayons and starts coloring on the kitchen table, a logical consequence would be, "If you can't keep the crayons on the paper, then I will have to take them away." If he continues to color on the table, then the crayons would have to be removed. However, they should be returned within half an hour to give him another opportunity to use them appropriately.

TODDLER ALERT
The principle is to make the consequence immediate, short, to the point and then quickly offer your child a chance to try again and be successful.

Positive Reminders

The key for children's learning is repeated positive learning trials and chances to try again and be successful.

Toddlers have a very short attention span and often have difficulty understanding verbal instructions. They will need frequent positive reminders of the limits and frequent praise whenever they remember to follow the rules. Remember, the key for children's learning is repeated positive learning trials and chances to try again and be successful. In the scenario we saw earlier, the father repeated his instruction, "Please sit down" or "Tush on seat" several times with some nonverbal signals. This repetition is important because toddlers may be distracted by something else going on or by their drive to explore and not process the verbal instruction being given to them.

Repeat instructions

Choosing Your Battles

In the next scenario a mother, father and their three-year-old son Robin and their five-year-old daughter Dorian are having dinner together. Think about how these parents choose their battles with each of their children—and think about what limits they decide to give and those commands they avoid giving in order to make their mealtime as enjoyable as possible.

Robin asks to sit with his father. Father tells Robin, "You can sit on my lap if you bring your food over and eat more food." Robin goes over to sit in his father's lap, bringing his plate. Dorian says, "I'm finished eating. Can I get down from the table now?" and her mother replies, "Thanks for asking so politely but we are all still eating so you need to sit a few minutes at the table, or Robin will leave too." She engages Dorian in a conversation about the card she made for her friend. Dorian starts rocking her head back and forth, singing loudly. Mother laughs at this and then Robin copies this singing and head rocking briefly and spills his milk. Mother ignores this and tells them, "In about three more minutes we will make whipped cream for dessert." Dorian argues that she wants to get up from the table right away and then starts rocking and singing again. This time mother ignores her actions. Robin says, "I'm done" and father checks with him and reminds him of the limit, "Do you have enough food in your tummy to last until breakfast? There will be no more food after dessert until breakfast." Robin says, "No thank you," and mother praises his polite manners. Mother says to Dorian. "Thank you for staying at the table, your three

minutes are up now, please clear your plate." Dorian gets up from the table taking her plate to the sink and mother comments, "You are doing a good job carrying your plate carefully to the sink; thank you for being so helpful."

Describe the 'positive opposite' behavior you want, not the negative behavior you don't want.

In this scenario we see the differing expectations that the parents have for each child and differing goals. For Robin their goal seems to be to give him enough opportunity to eat his dinner without the distraction of his sister leaving the table, which will result in him following her. Moreover, although the father would like Robin to eat in his own seat, he is willing to let him sit in his lap if that results in him eating more food. He gives him an opportunity to eat and a clear warning is given that after dessert there will be no more food until breakfast. It will be important that he follow through with that rule.

The father avoided giving unnecessary commands or corrections that could have resulted in a power struggle such as forcing him to stay seated in his chair and eat his food, or criticism for not eating, or spilling his milk on his pants. He gave him some autonomy but also let him know the rules about further eating.

In Dorian's case she has eaten quickly and wants to leave the table. Mother sets a clear limit, and explains why she needs to stay at the table (because Robin will leave and not eat) and tries to distract her with conversation about her art and the next day's activities. However, Dorian has discovered she can get more reaction and attention from the whole family by rocking and singing antics. This ends up being distracting for Robin who is intrigued by it and models it himself. If the parents wanted this behavior to stop they could have ignored it completely from the start and focused on something positive about Robin. However, it is helpful that they avoided being critical about the behavior itself.

Follow Clear Limit Setting with a Distraction

When parents give a command stopping a toddler from doing something, it can often be helpful to immediately divert or distract the child's attention in some way. This may prevent the child from protesting in anger and becoming disruptive. In the next scenario a mother and her two daughters are playing with measuring cups in a sandbox. Think about how the mother sets the limit and gets her four-year-old daughter, Ally, to help her to distract her toddler, Molly, from eating crayons.

When you give a command stopping a toddler from doing something, it can be helpful to immediately divert or distract the child's attention.

Mother says, "Molly, put the crayon down. Crayons are not to eat." She immediately takes the crayon away and turns to the four-year-old daughter, Ally, saying, "Is there something else that Molly can chew on?" The mother begins to give Molly a yellow cup but Ally protests, "I need that one."

Mother responds, "Ally, can you find something else for Molly that she can chew on?" Ally replies, "She can play with this. I don't need this." Mother hands Molly the measuring cup and says, "Molly, you can play with this one, Ally is sharing with you, that is friendly and it is a nice one with pretty colors."

In this scenario the mother uses a verbal command and then a distraction to keep Molly from chewing on crayons. Because the little girl is so young, the mother does not expect her to comply with her initial command to put the crayon down. Instead she follows through by gently taking the crayon away and substituting a different toy that the little girl can chew on. The mother maximizes this learning experience for her older daughter by asking her what toy her little sister can chew and when she decides which one to share with her, she helps Molly understand what it means to share, in so doing making Ally feel proud.

I use distractions after a command

Expecting and Handling Protests

Encouraging your toddler's autonomy, choosing your battles, and setting clear and polite limits does not mean your toddler won't get frustrated or angry when she feels her explorations are thwarted. Some may call this misbehavior but actually toddlers are not deliberately trying to disobey, rather they are overwhelmed by their own developmental curiosity and urges to explore. Don't be alarmed by this, in fact expect it as normal part of a toddler's development. Be prepared to ignore all protests and arguments as you follow through with the limit and remain calm and patient as your toddler finds out what she has control over and what she does not have control over. In the next scenario think about how the mother is limit setting and handling her daughter's protests.

> Be prepared to ignore all protests and arguments as you follow through with the limit.

Jolie, an 18-month-old tries to climb onto the coffee table. The mother sets a limit, "Keep your feet on the floor. The table is not for climbing." Mother moves Jolie back down to the floor. Jolie cries. Mother calmly explains again, "Your feet need to be on the floor. Climbing isn't safe. You can use your truck on the table." Jolie tries again to climb on the table and mother says, "No— don't climb on the table. I know you are frustrated but you can't climb up." Jolie sucks her thumb unhappily as mother gently moves her down again. Her mother picks her up and walks away from the table, "Let's find something else to play with."

As we can see, this little girl's developmental need to climb on and explore the table interfered with her understanding of why her mother was telling her "no." As the scenario continues think about how the mother uses an engaging redirect to help divert Jolie's need to explore to some other activity and to help her self-regulate her emotions.

Mother brings out a baby dinosaur puppet and explains, "It looks like a frog but it is not a frog, it is a dinosaur" and Jolie repeats the word dinosaur. Mother tells her, "The dinosaur is in an egg" and then has the baby dinosaur kiss her and tells her, "Baby dinosaur loves you." Jolie kisses the baby dinosaur back. Mother comments, "That is so sweet" and makes the dinosaur kiss her again. Mother describes Jolie's changed emotion, "Now you are happy." The dinosaur talks to Jolie and she smiles. The dinosaur says, "You look happy." Jolie sings and appears content. She has completely forgotten about the table.

One of the best ways to say no to a toddler is with actions rather than words.

In this scenario it is evident that the mother's distraction or redirection was more effective than her "no" command or explanation of why she couldn't go onto the table. Then we also see how this mother emphasized how Jolie's sad feelings could change to happy feelings when doing something else using some emotion coaching.

We have talked earlier about reducing "no commands" when possible. Of course, there are times when it is necessary to say "no." When you do so, remember some of the following points for helping your toddler cope with their frustration about this:

Dealing with "No"

- Redirect or distract your toddler with something else very interesting.
- Remove the forbidden object in some way (cover with blanket, put up high or take out of room).
- Give a direction that tells your toddler what she CAN do, rather than what she can't do.
- Offer limited choices to your toddler when possible.
- Respond with humor or a song.
- Turn tasks into games, for example, "fly" to the bathroom or make a "train" to the bedroom.
- Don't give a lot of attention to the toddler's "no"– ignore, redirect, or change the subject so it is not reinforced.
- Tell your toddler "yes" when you can.

This does not mean a parent can never say no. However, one of the best ways to say no to a toddler is with actions rather than words. For example, immediately take away the object that is misused, separate the children when there is hitting, move the child to another place in the room if she is touching something she shouldn't, or hold her hand so she can't run in the street. Remember actions speak louder than words, as children do not process parents' verbal reasoning very well.

TODDLER ALERT

Constant parent vigilance is needed in order to keep your toddler safe. Monitor constantly. Remember, actions speak louder than words.

Praising Compliance and Cooperation with Requests

Do you praise your toddler for following your directions or do you ignore this and take it for granted? Perhaps one of the most essential components of teaching your toddler to begin to cooperate with your requests is giving your children specific praise when they listen to you and do what you ask. This encouragement on your part will increase the likelihood your children will be cooperative and will value your requests. On the other hand, if there is no follow-through with enthusiastic praise, then you can expect your requests to be ignored in the future.

Specific praise

Avoid Unclear or Question Commands

Some parents have trouble because they make too many commands. However, there are other parents who dislike limit setting and feel guilty when they say no. Often these parents are vague and indirect about rules and disguise their commands in some fashion, perhaps to ease

their guilt. Think about what a toddler understands she is being asked to do when she hears her parent make requests such as, "Now, be careful," "quit it," "cut it out," "in a minute," "watch out," "be good," or "act right." Commands or limits that are unclear or vague, will be confusing to toddlers. Remember, if the request doesn't clearly specify the positive behavior that you want, your toddler won't know what to do.

A second type of request that is problematic for children is a question command. Think about what your toddler understands you are asking her to do if you say, "Hey, I think we are going to eat, why don't you come and wash your hands?" "Do you think it is time for bed now?" or "Why don't you put away the toys now?" Parents often phrase commands as a question as if they are giving their toddler a choice as to whether or not to comply. Then if their child says "No" they are trapped by this response. When this happens, the parent might wind up doing the task (such as putting away the toys) rather than trying to persuade the child to do it. This can backfire because the parent is reinforcing the child for her noncompliance. If you expect your child to comply and there is not choice, then phrase it as a clear command not a question.

If the request doesn't clearly specify the positive behavior that you want, your toddler won't know what to do.

Avoid Negative Requests or Commands

A third type of parental request that is ineffective is a request given with an angry voice and/or including a criticism or negative comment with the request. For example, a father and his two sons are at the table having a snack and the father looks over at this son and says, "I told you about eating like a little pig, Whitney, having crumbs and stuff around your mouth." The boy responds by shrugging his shoulders. This father's approach is not an effective way to change his son's behavior, and his comments about

Polite requests

eating "like a little pig" might either make the child feel bad about himself or cause him to imitate a pig. It is not clear what the father wants his son to do to drink or eat correctly. Stating the request in a more positive way by saying, "Whitney, please lift the glass carefully with two hands," or "Please wipe the crumbs from your mouth," would be more effective at teaching the boy what positive behavior is expected of him.

Try to avoid criticizing your child when setting a limit or making a request, because your child's feelings about herself as a worthwhile person should be considered at least as important as getting his cooperation. A child who feels bad or worthless will tend to act that way.

Make Reasonable Requests

It is important when making requests of young children to have realistic and age appropriate expectations. For example, asking a toddler to get completely dressed by herself, button up her shirt, clean up a whole room of toys, follow a multi-step direction, or to make her bed is too physically complex and advanced a skill for this age. When asking your toddler to do something, make sure your child has the developmental ability to do the task.

Use Clear Respectful Commands

In the next scenario think about all the ways this mother is effective in the way she sets a limit with her two-year-old daughter.

Mother tells her daughter, Soleil, in a respectful but firm tone, "You may ride your tricycle on the side walk but not on the road." She explains, "Riding on the street it isn't safe." She repeats the limit again while pointing out the areas she can and cannot ride and saying, "Soleil, you can ride here by the grass on the side walk, not there on the road." Through this simple direction she gets eye contact with her daughter and finishes by saying, "Good listening to the rules about biking." The little girl goes off riding on the sidewalk and her mother watches and monitors her to be sure she is safe. After a few moments she goes up to her again and says enthusiastically, "You are doing a great job of staying on the side walk and not going too far away, you are getting to be a big girl." She continues to watch her and stay nearby.

This mother is staying calm, respectful and clear in her expectations. Moreover, she doesn't expect her verbal instructions to be understood by her child. Instead, she stays to watch and monitor whether her toddler understands how to follow the instructions and is ready to give attention and praise her behavior when she shows she knows what to do. In essence she combines a behavioral practice along side the verbal directions.

Transition Commands/Warnings

Some parents give commands abruptly, without any warning. Picture this scene, Anna is totally absorbed in building a tower with her Duplos. Suddenly mother comes in the room and tells her to go to bed. What happens next? Probably much unhappiness, protesting and resistance from Anna.

I give transition warnings

It is helpful to prepare children for transitions such as ending play, or going to bed by giving a warning that their activity will be ending soon.

Children who are engaged in an interesting activity will often dysregulate if the activity is ended abruptly without warning. When feasible, it is helpful to prepare children for transitions such as ending play, going to bed, leaving a friend's house, or turning off the TV by giving a warning that their activity will be ending soon. You can pair this transition warning with a reminder of what will happen next. In the next scenario, notice how the mother uses transition warnings to help her two children transition from playtime to bedtime.

Mother gives a transition warning, "We're going to play for three more minutes and then it will be teeth time and time for stories in bed." Robin, a three-year-old is busy playing and seems not to hear the warning. Mother repeats the warning by looking him in face and getting his attention. She says, "Robin three more minutes of play time and then it will be teeth and stories." A little later she gives the one-minute warning, "one more minute of play and it will be teeth time and story time." Then she gives the command, "It's time to clean up the toys for teeth." She waits a minute for the children to comply and they seem to ignore her. She starts with her follow through by saying, "Here's a box, it is time to put these away, and we can play with these tomorrow morning." Robin puts a toy in the box and mother says, "Thank you Robin for putting that away." Mother herself models by starting to put some away herself and thanks Dorian who is cleaning up more quickly than Robin. Dorian asks her, "Do we have to put our structure away?" and mother replies, "You can close the box, lay it on top and play with it some more tomorrow." Mother thanks Dorian for finishing cleaning up. Robin has started playing again. Mother follows through by moving Robin's hand with the toy in it to the

box and thanking him for putting it away. Next Robin takes something out of the box he says he needs and mother says, "You can save it for the bus for tomorrow, put it on top of the toy box." Mother thanks him and says, "Say good night to your toy" which he does and she thanks him again for helping clean up, "Good work for helping cleaning up, now lets see if we can take a train ride to the bathroom."

In this scenario, we can appreciate all the work on the part of this mother to stay patient, calm and to give clear instructions. She gives good warning statements that their play activity will end soon and helps them understand what will happen next. She follows through by physically moving Robin's hand with the toy in it to the box and uses herself as a model to show what behavior is expected. She also gives them some choice by not requiring their structure be taken apart when put away, but allows them to save it for the next day. She does not become frustrated with Robin's resistance and helps him with the transition by saying good-bye to the toys.

There are many ways to give warnings. For young children who don't understand the concept of time like Robin, a buzzer, timer, or music can be a helpful signal to let children know that the time is almost up for something to end. You can say, "When the timer goes off, it will be time to put the blocks away." For older preschool

Stay calm, patient and relaxed

children you can refer to a clock. For example, you can say, "When the big hand gets to the seven, it will be time to put away the blocks and get on the train for bed." A warning connected to a specific activity can also be helpful. For example, "We will read one more book and then it will be time to turn out the light." Or, "You can build one more tower to knock over, and then you need to clean up." If you are consistent with your warnings, over time, your children will learn to begin preparing to end an activity when they hear your transition cue.

Maintaining Self-Control

Many family members find that in stressful situations they cannot maintain their self-control. Others report they suffer from chronic anger, anxiety or depression, and they are easily set off by the slightest event. However, when parents allow themselves to become so overwhelmed that they overreact, the consequences can be unfortunate. Parents may say or do something they will regret. After they calm down, they may feel guilty and avoid dealing with the child for fear of repeating the episode. It is frightening and anxiety-provoking for a child to see a parent lose control. Also, the child learns to imitate these aggressive behaviors in other situations. These cycles of parental overreaction and avoidance make it difficult to deal with the child in a consistent manner.

The best approach is to try to stay calm, patient and relaxed. You can do this by using calming and coping thoughts and stopping your negative thoughts so you are not so overwhelmed that you can't respond or so upset you overreact.

Here is an example if you find yourself thinking, "I can't handle this when he's angry, he never obeys," tell yourself, " I can handle this. I can cope with this. He's just testing the limits and trying to get control. I can be patient, ignore this, redirect him, and help him learn low to us his words." Controlling your negative thoughts will lead to more positive feelings and more effective parenting. We will discuss this more in Chapter 7.

To Sum Up...

So we have seen that limit setting with toddlers requires constant supervision and monitoring to ensure their safety. Learning to give toddlers clear requests and commands that describe the positive behavior that you want instead of the negative behavior you don't want can be a new language for many parents. But it is well worth the effort in terms of your child's positive responses. We have also learned about the importance of thinking carefully before giving a command to be sure it's necessary and you are prepared to follow through with it with some action. It's important to strike a balance between a child's choices and drive for autonomy and parent rules and limits. However, keeping calm, staying patient and modeling respectful behavior is key to eventual success with children because children learn more by watching parental behavior than by what parents tell children to do (actions speak louder than words). Giving effective commands is harder than you might first expect. Warnings, choices, redirections, when-then commands and transitions help children cope with having limits set on their behavior but most of all praise for compliance to instructions and commands will make all the difference.

Monitoring toddler

Points to Remember about
TODDLER LIMIT SETTING

- Constant supervision of toddlers is essential to their safety.
- Don't give unnecessary requests.
- Give one command or request at a time.
- Be realistic in your expectations and use age-appropriate requests.
- Use "do" commands that detail the desired positive behavior. Keep them to three words with the action verb first.
- Make requests positive and polite.
- Limit use of "stop" or "no" commands.
- All children need time to respond to requests: Wait to give another command or request until your child has complied or five seconds have passed.
- Give warnings and helpful reminders.
- Don't threaten children; use "when-then" requests.
- Avoid using "let's" commands, chain commands, question commands, negative commands and vague commands.
- Give children choices whenever possible.
- Make requests short and to the point.
- Support your partner's requests.
- Praise compliance or provide consequences for noncompliance.
- Strike a balance between parent and child control.
- Use redirections or distraction to help refocus child after s/he has been prohibited from doing something.

pervise toddler

Parents' Viewpoint
MY COPING THOUGHTS JOURNAL

Write down here some positive coping thoughts you will use to stay calm when your are frustrated with your toddler's behavior.

Positive thoughts I will practice:

Goal:

I will commit to tell myself the following when I am getting frustrated:

_____

Parents' Viewpoint
OUR FAMILY RULES JOURNAL

Write down what you think are your most important household rules. Post these on your refrigerator so that your baby sitters and other family members will know what they are. Take pictures of your child following these rules and post these on your rules poster and/or in your journal.

Some Examples:

1. Bedtime is at 7:30 p.m.

2. Keep hands to self -No hitting allowed.

3. Sit in back of car in car seat.

4. Trike riding is only allowed on the sidewalk, not in the street.

List of My Household Rules:

1.

2.

3.

4.

Every home needs a limited number of "house rules."
If the list gets too long, no one will remember the rules.

MY LIMIT SETTING JOURNAL

Write down the benefits of having clear limits and your difficulties in doing it. See if you can find any solutions to your barriers to setting clear limits.

BENEFIT OF SETTING LIMITS	DIFFICULTIES IN DOING THIS

Solutions

Write an approach you will take to overcome your barriers.

Goal:

I will commit to reducing the number of commands or requests to those that are most important. Instead, I will focus on giving choices when possible, using distractions and when-then commands.

Parents' Viewpoint
MY LIMIT SETTING LANGUAGE

Rewrite the following ineffective commands into positive, clear, respectful commands or requests. At the end of this list write in the less effective commands you notice you frequently use and then rewrite these to the positive opposite. Practice these replacement words when limit setting and notice the difference in your toddler's response.

Negative Commands	Rewrite Positive Command
Shut up	
Quit shouting	
Stop running	
Watch it	
Why don't we go to bed?	
Let's clean up the living room	
Cut it out	

Negative Commands	Rewrite Positive Command
What is your coat doing there?	
Why are your shoes in the living room?	
Don't shove salad in your mouth like a pig	
Why are you still crying?	
You look like a mess	
Stop yelling	
You are never ready	
Your clothes are filthy	
This room is a mess	
Don't whine	

Negative Commands	Rewrite Positive Command
You are impossible	
Stop dawdling	
Hurry up	
Why are you riding on the road when you've been told not to?	
I'll hit you if you do that again	

Your Negative Commands

Parents' Viewpoint
THOUGHT CONTROL JOURNAL

Researchers have demonstrated that there is a relationship between how we think, feel and how we behave. For example, if you view the child in hostile terms ("He is misbehaving because—he likes to get me upset"), you are likely to become very angry. On the other hand, if your thoughts emphasize your ability to cope ("I'm going to have to help him learn to control himself"), this will help to bring about more patient, rational and effective responses. One of the first steps for improving the way you think about your child is to replace upsetting thoughts and negative self-statements with positive calming and coping thoughts.

Write your own positive coping thought statements and practice them during the week.

MY TODDLER'S PICTURE

Take a picture of your child following one of your rules such as wearing a seat belt or tricycle helmet.

CHAPTER 7

Positive Discipline—
Handling Misbehavior

Introduction

Now we have gotten to the top of the parenting pyramid and indeed it is very important for parents and other child care providers or teachers to know how to respond to children's misbehavior. For even when parents are using all the proactive strategies discussed earlier, all children behave inappropriately sometimes, and having effective strategies for dealing with these misbehaviors is crucial. However, you will notice that these parenting strategies are used far less often than all the other foundational strategies at the bottom of the pyramid. If your parenting pyramid has a solid positive foundation, you will have less need for the discipline strategies at the top of the pyramid.

It may surprise parents to know that as long as your child is safe and not hurting someone else, the best parental response to many misbehaviors is to completely ignore them. In prior chapters we have discussed the powerful impact that parental

attention, coaching, and praise has on strengthening the brain connections that affect children's development of positive academic, social behavior and emotional competence. We've also talked about how lack of parental attention, or ignoring, leads to decreases in children's misbehavior. In this chapter, we will discuss the implications of using this "attention principle" for decreasing children's attention-seeking negative behaviors. These are behaviors like whining, throwing a tantrum, screaming, fussing, rude talk, and any many other annoying or disruptive behaviors. In this chapter parents will learn to use planned ignoring to reduce those types of problem behaviors, while giving attention to the "positive opposite" behaviors that they would like to see instead (asking nicely, accepting no, staying calm, using a grown up voice).

Positive attention

Objections to Ignoring

Frequently parents feel uncomfortable with the idea of ignoring misbehavior. Their objections range from worries that they are neglecting their child if they don't respond, to the fear that ignoring is not enough of a consequence to a behavior that is problematic. Here are some common questions or concerns that parents ask about using the ignore approach.

Isn't ignoring children's misbehavior unrealistic and irresponsible?

"I just can't see ignoring a child when he or she is throwing a tantrum, running around, not listening or yelling at you. Why let a child do that? These behaviors need discipline!"

Frequently parents don't feel that ignoring is sufficient discipline when a child is displaying a problem behavior. Remember that the word "discipline" means "to teach." So, ignoring is actually a very effective form of discipline. Ignoring teaches children that there is no payoff (such as parental attention, interactions, or power struggles) for inappropriate behaviors. When parents do not visibly react to these misbehaviors, children lose their motivation for continuing to use them. Children will learn that throwing a tantrum doesn't get a reaction and doesn't result in what they

The word "discipline" means "to teach." So, ignoring is actually a very effective form of discipline.

I pair ignoring misbehavior with attention for the positive opposite behavior

want. If parents pair ignoring with positive attention and approval for appropriate behaviors, children begin to substitute positive behaviors for their negative ones in order to get their attention that way. Moreover, when a parent ignores instead of yelling at or criticizing the child, the parent is modeling for the child the ability to maintain self-control in the face of conflict and anger, an effective model for emotional regulation. This also maintains a positive parent-child relationship where discipline is based on respect rather than fear.

Am I abandoning my child if I ignore her when she is distressed?

"It upsets me to see my child cry when I tell her 'no.' I'm afraid that she will think I don't care about her any more or that I am abandoning her because she is upset."

No parent likes to see their child distressed, and frequently, when children are disappointed or are told "no" they are genuinely distressed. This means that there is real emotion behind their tears and tantrums, but if you respond to this negative emotion, you are sending your child the message that tears and anger are an appropriate way to get what she wants. Remember that we are talking about a planned ignore wherein you are close by and only ignoring until your child has regained control of her emotions. Then you return your attention to her. There are many appropriate times to register your understanding and empathy for your child's distress, which we will discuss later in the chapter.

> We are talking about a planned ignore wherein you are close by and only ignoring until your child has regained control.

 TODDLER ALERT

Ignoring is an inappropriate discipline response for some difficult behaviors, so you would not ignore a child who is hurt, scared, worried, or sad (unless the sadness is because you've calmly refused to buy her a toy at the store).

How long should you ignore?

"I can ignore for only so long–then I explode and yell at him."

Sometimes well-intentioned parents start to ignore misbehavior such as tantrums or protests without being prepared for their child's response. Most children, when ignored, will initially react with an increase in negative behaviors. They believe that if they can yell long enough or loud enough, their parents will eventually give in and respond. For instance, three-year-old Megan tantrums because her mother won't let her go outside. Megan escalates her tantrums to see if she can get what she wants. This goes on for five more minutes until her mother, exasperated and worn down by the tantrum, says, "All right, go outside!" By giving in for the short-term benefit of making life more peaceful, the mother has created a long-term problem. Megan has learned that if she tantrums long and hard enough, she will get what she wants. Thus, her tantrum behavior has been reinforced.

Remember when you first start ignoring a misbehavior, it will usually get worse. If you are going to use this approach—which is powerfully effective—your must be prepared to wait out this period if the behavior is to improve. If you give in, your child will learn that persisting in the misbehavior is an effective way to get what she wants. It is actually better to give in immediately than it is to begin to ignore and then give in after your child has worn you down.

What if I am ignoring my child but others are not?

"I tried ignoring his tantrums, but all the other children in child care laugh at him and his grandmother comforts him when he begins to tantrum—so what good does it do for me to ignore?"

This is an important point. If the child's misbehavior is being reinforced or given attention by other children or adults in the room, then the ignoring is probably going to be ineffective. In such a case, the parent may need to remove the child to another place where the ignoring can be carried out effectively. Parents may also want to consider informing relatives, baby-sitters, neighbors, or teachers about the plan to ignore targeted misbehaviors. If parents can get the cooperation of relatives and teachers to ignore selected annoying behaviors the strategy will be much more effective.

I teach other family members behaviors to ignore

How can you ignore a child who clings onto you?

"I find that when I ignore his tantrums and yelling, he gets worse and starts to pull on my body and follow me around screaming. It drives me crazy and I explode."

When ignoring a clinging child, it may help for the parent to physically move away—to stand up and walk to another part of the same room. If the child follows, it may be helpful for the parent to remain standing up

Ignore tantrums

(so that the child only has access to boring feet and legs). If the parent pretends to read a magazine or starts to do kitchen chores, it will be evident to the child that the screaming and tantrumming is not working to get their attention. By staying near by the parent can monitor their child's behavior and reinforce him as soon as he stops misbehaving.

Threatening the ultimate ignore?

"Okay, I decided to use the ultimate ignore. He wouldn't get dressed and I asked him a hundred times so I finally said, "If you don't get your shoes, on I will leave without you." Well, he wasn't ready so I got in the car and drove down the street. When I came back he was dressed and standing crying on the street—so it worked."

Parents who take ignoring to an extreme and threaten to leave their children or actually do pretend to leave believe that fear will mobilize the children into being more compliant. While such threats may work in the short run to get a child out the door, they have several long-term disadvantages. In order to continue to be effective, all threats need to be backed up with the threatened consequence. Once a child realizes the parent is only pretending to leave, he will respond with similar threats saying, "Go ahead and leave me. See if I care!" The parent is then left in a powerless position because the child has called his/her bluff. To not leave is to fail to follow through. Yet leaving isn't really an option, since a young child is not safe alone at home. The emotional hazard is also great, as threats to abandon children make them feel insecure and lead to poor self-esteem. Furthermore, parents are providing a powerful model, namely, avoiding conflict by running away from it. When the child is older, he will have learned to begin threatening to run away or even leave home to test the power of this tactic for getting what he wants.

Never threaten to leave or abandon your children, no matter how great the temptation. There are more effective strategies for inducing compliance. If you can muster the self-control to ignore the behavior that makes you feel so angry, your child will begin to behave more appropriately, and your frustration will decrease. When ignoring isn't feasible another discipline technique such as a logical consequence may be called for. While these strategies will take more of parents' time and emotional patience in the short run, they teach children that the parent-child relationship is secure, regardless of conflict. These strategies are far preferable because they are based on respect, rather than on fear of abandonment.

**Promoting
security**

Ignoring Misbehavior

Now that we have covered some of the common concerns parents have about ignoring, it's time to talk about the practicalities of using ignoring effectively as a strategy for reducing misbehavior.

First, it is important to remember that ignoring will decrease negative behaviors, but will not teach children what to do instead. Therefore ignoring is always paired with other strategies that are designed to teach the positive opposite or replacement prosocial behaviors. In other words, if a parent is ignoring her child's whining, she will also be coaching and praising other behaviors such as "asking in a big boy, polite voice" and "using a calm, friendly voice."

It is also important to try to prevent misbehavior from occurring in the first place. By now you have already learned many parenting strategies for preventing misbehavior or nipping it in the bud before it escalates. Through toddler-centered play, coaching, parent modeling, and praise you are strengthening your toddler's social and emotional competence, building a strong positive relationship, and encouraging your toddler's autonomy. An outburst can often be prevented by giving the child a little support and encouragement before he becomes frustrated and misbehaves. Distraction or redirection can prevent misbehavior when a conflict is first developing

> Ignoring will decrease negative behaviors, but will not teach children what to do instead.

TODDLER ALERT

Try to be patient because outbursts are a normal part of toddlers' developmental drive to explore and develop their sense of self.

between two children who are playing together. By setting up predictable routines, giving clear, positive commands and reducing the number of commands you give, and by using distractions and redirections you are helping your child feel safe and learn to trust the world. Even though you do all these things, toddlers will still misbehave and test the limits to see if they are secure. In the next scenario, think about how the mother tries to prepare her two-year old daughter for a transition, and how she responds when her child is not ready to clean up. Think about how she handles this behavior.

Mother says to Brooke, "We're going to have dinner in a few more minutes, Brooke. It is almost time to put the books away." (transition warning) A few minutes later, she says to Brooke, "Put the book away. Go put the book on the shelf." (clear command) Brooke whines, fusses and holds the book tightly protesting, "No, no, bunny book." The mother says, "Put the book away and we'll get some juice." (distraction and redirection) Brooke screams loudly, "Oh, no, no, no. No, mine!" Mother takes the book away from Brooke and picks her up and ignores her screaming by looking away. Brooke continues to scream loudly. Mother continues turning her head away, avoids eye contact and makes no further comment. Brooke looks for her mother's response, and when she doesn't get it she stops screaming and soothes herself with her thumb. At this point, Brooke's mother says, "Good girl to calm down. Let's go get our juice."

This mother does a good job of first giving a transition warning, then, when Brooke is upset with the command to put the book away, she tries a redirection. This is often a very effective technique with toddlers. However, Brooke continues to protest and begins to tantrum. The mother is clear, assertive, positive, and follows through with the command when it is clear that Brooke is not going to be pacified with the offer to go get juice after the book is put away. She realizes that in order to follow through with her command, she will need to physically take the book away from Brooke. She does this as calmly as possible, turning her head away and avoiding eye contact so that her ignore is clear and complete. As soon as Brooke is calm again, the mother returns her attention, praising Brooke for her calm body and helping her move on to another activity. Although Brooke is directing a great deal of anger toward the parent when she is not allowed to do something, it should not be interpreted as a personal attack. She is merely testing to see if the rule is going to be enforced consistently. By effectively ignoring, Brooke's mother is reinforcing the limit that she set, and is also helping Brooke learn to calm down when frustrated. This is an early self-regulation skill!

Follow through with limits

Avoid Discussion and Eye Contact

Your facial expression should be neutral, you should avoid eye contact, and stop all discussions.

Sometimes parents think they're ignoring their children's misbehavior when they are actually giving it considerable attention. They may have stopped talking to their child but continue to glare, grimace, or in other ways let their child know that the misbehavior is affecting them. Some parents ignore by avoiding eye contact with their child but continue to make critical or corrective comments. In both instances, the misbehaving child is successful in getting attention and, perhaps, a powerful negative emotional response as well.

Effective ignoring occurs when you are able to minimize your reaction to what your child is doing. Your facial expression should be neutral, you should avoid eye contact, and stop all discussions with your toddler. Ignoring also involves moving away from the child, especially if you have been in close contact. Just as the most powerful form of positive attention includes a smile, eye contact, verbal praise and physical touching, the most powerful form of ignoring is a neutral expression, involving no eye contact, no communication, and a turning away of the body.

Coping with No! No! No!
Avoid Responding with Corrections or Commands

Often when children misbehave, parents respond by giving a command, yelling, giving a criticism, or making a correction. Often this response may prolong the misbehavior, and instead it is better to ignore the misbehavior altogether. Remember, the rationale for ignoring is straightforward. Children's behavior is maintained by the attention it receives. Even negative attention such as parental nagging, yelling, and criticizing is reinforcing children's misbehavior. When ignoring misbehavior, there is no "pay off" to continue to misbehave, and so the child will eventually stop. In the next scenario, think about the commands and strategies the same mother is using to get Brooke to stop touching and playing with the TV.

The rationale for ignoring is straightforward. Children's behavior is maintained by the attention it receives.

Mother says, "No, Brooke, you may not touch the TV." She tries to move Brooke away from the TV. Brooke screams, "No! No! No!" Mother says, "We're not going to play with the TV. Here's a book you can look at." Brooke is not interested in the book and returns to the television set. Mother says, "We're not going to play with the TV. You may look at the TV, but you may not touch it." Brooke responds by whining and screaming a little louder. Mother tries to distract her, "Would you like to do some rocking now?" Brooke continues to play with the television set and ignores her. Mother repeats the command, "No, you may not play with the TV set. Would you like to do some rocking?" Brooke stays by the TV set, touching the buttons and fussing.

Initially Brooke's mother gave her a clear command not to touch the TV. This was a reasonable limit to set. Not surprisingly, Brooke did not respond to the command. Think back to chapter 6 on effective limit setting. What do you think Brooke is learning from her mother's repeated commands not to touch the TV? Perhaps she is learning that the commands don't mean very much, since she is still able to touch the buttons. She may also be learning that each time she touches the buttons, she gets a response from her mother. This can be a powerful feeling for a toddler! The mother also offered the suggestion to look but not touch, which is a command that might work for a five-year-old who has some self-regulation skills, but not for a toddler driven to explore. Next watch how this mother changes her limit-setting strategy.

Finally, the mother picks up Brooke, moves her away from the television set, and puts her on the rocking chair. Brooke responds with a loud, shrill scream. The mother turns away, avoids looking at her daughter and stops talking to her. Within a few seconds Brooke stops screaming. Brooke whimpers, "Can I have a book?" Mother quickly turns her attention back to Brooke and gives her the book saying, "Here's a book like we have. It's a book about animals." She turns the page saying, "These are cows and cows go 'Moo.'" Brooke sits quietly looking at the book. Mother says, "Beautiful. Such a good girl you are to sit and rock." Brooke says, happily, "Bunny! Bunny!"

This time mother realizes that distractions and repeating commands are not going to work, so she follows through by physically moving Brooke away from the TV. Then she effectively ignores Brooke's mini-tantrum by immediately withdrawing eye contact and verbal contact, and moving away so that Brooke gets no physical contact. She is not baffled by her toddler's screaming, stays calm and follows through by removing Brooke from the television. As soon as Brooke stops screaming and begins to behave appropriately, the mother immediately gives her attention. When Brooke is quiet, the mother is enthusiastic, praises her and uses distraction with success. From this interaction Brooke learns that her mother is willing to follow through with her command despite screaming and protests. The child also learns that there is no payoff for screaming, but on the other hand, quiet behavior does receive her attention and praise.

TODDLER ALERT

After ignoring, remember, it is essential that you are ready to give back your full attention to your child just as soon as your child calms down and stops misbehaving. Your positive attention at this time will help your child learn to self-regulate and will reinforce calming down. No ignore is complete until you give back your attention for positive behavior.

Behavior Gets Worse Before It Gets Better

Remember, when you first start ignoring a misbehavior it will usually get worse. You must be prepared to wait out this screaming period if the behavior is to improve. If you give in to tantrums, you will be reinforcing this behavior and your toddler will learn that by crying and screaming loudly he can get his own way. When your toddler was a baby, it was important to respond to crying because your baby had no other way to communicate his needs. However, during toddler years, your child must learn now that throwing a tantrum won't work to get what he wants, but instead using words and staying regulated will get his parents' response.

However, particularly if you are ignoring a behavior for the first time, it is likely that your child will test your ignoring powers at first. He will believe that if he is loud enough or persistent enough, that surely you will hear and respond. The analogy of buying a drink from a quirky vending machine is helpful here. You put your change in for a soft drink, but don't get one, nor can you get your money back. You press the return button several times and when this doesn't work you try the drink button again. Depending on how thirsty or cross you are, you may persist in pressing the buttons and even try banging on the machine. Finally, if no soft drink appears, you give up and move on to something else because there has been no payoff for your banging (the machine ignored you until you gave up!). You are also unlikely to waste your money in this machine again. However, if by some stroke of luck a soft drink pops out during your banging, then you know that the next time you can't get a soft drink from that machine, the trick is to bang hard and long enough. Children can learn to be persistent bangers. This is one of the reasons that ignoring is so difficult for parents to carry out. All children will test their parents' ignoring skills by escalating their misbehaviors. If you decide to use the ignoring technique you must be prepared to wait out this period by remaining firm in your resolution to ignore.

All children will test their parents' ignoring skills by escalating their misbehaviors.

Pairing a Distraction with Ignoring

Limit setting
+
distraction

Choosing to ignore misbehavior doesn't mean that there is nothing positive you can do to improve the situation. In fact, failure to provide distractions or suggestions for alternative, more appropriate behavior can lock parents and children into a power struggle and cause the children to prolong the misbehaviors. For young children, pairing your limit setting with a distraction can be a very useful way to shorten a temper tantrum.

The trick is to time the distraction so that it has the most chance of working and so that it's not being offered as response to the tantrum. You might first offer a preemptive distraction. For example, your toddler has the TV remote, which is not acceptable. Father finds a colorful rattle and tries to trade the remote for the rattle. If this works, then a power struggle has been averted, and the child doesn't even realize that a limit has been set.

If the child objects to the trade, which often happens, then the parent sets the limit and follows through, by removing the remote and saying, "You can play with the rattle, but not the remote." If the child tantrums in response to the removal of the remote, then the father ignores until he is calmer. If he continues to try to distract him when he is crying, he will be reinforcing his crying. At the point when the child is calm again, the father can reintroduce a distraction by saying, "Let's go to your room and find something to play with." If the father continued to ignore, even after his son is calm, he is likely to begin to scream again, perhaps search for the remote, or find some other unacceptable activity to engage in.

Another way to combine distraction with ignoring is to distract yourself from your children's inappropriate behaviors. You can do this by talking to yourself or another person, or involving yourself in another activity. If you are ignoring a child who is having a tantrum, you may want to go over to the kitchen sink and peel potatoes, or you might comment on something that is occurring outside the kitchen window or you might listen to music. If your child thinks you have been distracted, he may quickly stop misbehaving.

When Distractions Don't Work

Sometimes when you are prohibiting a toddler from doing something he wants to do, your distractions may not seem to work. In the next scenario Patrick, a 12-month-old wants to go in another room but his mother has indicated this room is off limits because of a project she doesn't want disrupted. Think about what Patrick may be learning from his parent's repeated attempts to distract him.

Patrick tries to go into the forbidden area and Mother follows through by picking him up and bringing him back to the play area. Patrick tantrums and his mother holds him and Father tries to distract him with music. Patrick's mother then puts him down while he continues to tantrum. However, Father picks him up and hugs him telling him it is okay. Patrick continues screaming and Father tries another  *distraction, a stuffed doggie, but this doesn't work. The parents try a variety of things to distract Patrick but he is angry and hits the airplane toy which they have offered him. Patrick continues crying. Mother gives him a kiss. She tries to pick him up again but he won't regulate. He goes back over to the forbidden room and this time Father brings him back. First Father tries rocking him and then he puts him on his knee and tries the motorcycle game. Patrick continues to scream and Mother suggests getting him some water and crackers. He continues crying. Father tries rocking again and then some Lego toys. She hands him some crackers saying he can have some if he wants but he doesn't have to. He takes a cracker while continuing to cry.*

These parents have done a great job of staying calm and trying to help their son self-regulate. They have tried many strategies to help him self-regulate such as hugging, rocking, music, soothing words, and distractions to more interesting toys and food. None of these distractions seem to be working and their continued attention on his misbehavior is likely serving to reinforce his tantrums rather than stop them. After you have made some good efforts to distract and help your child self-soothe, then the next strategy is to ignore the tantrum and let the child get himself under control. As soon as Patrick is calm and regulated then the parents should immediately give him their attention.

After you have made some good efforts to distract and help your child self-soothe, then the next strategy is to ignore the tantrum.

Help toddlers self-regulate and give them enough time

Move Away from Your Child but Stay in the Room

It may seem reasonable to ignore your child's misbehaviors by walking out of the room, especially if your child is clinging and physically demanding attention. However, the difficulty with leaving the room is that you won't be able to monitor your toddler's behavior nor will you be there when it is time to give your attention back to the appropriate behavior. When ignoring, it is best to physically move away by standing up and walking to another part of the room. This way you can monitor your child's behavior and reinforce him as soon as he stops misbehaving.

TODDLER ALERT

Remember—even with all your prevention strategies, toddlers will still tantrum and need to develop the self regulation skills to calm down.

Focus on Being Calm

When children misbehave and are tantrumming, parents often feel discouraged and helpless or, angry, and frustrated. Upsetting feelings are normal and to be expected. However, it is important you don't let your negative feelings so overwhelm you that you are immobilized by inaction or lose control of your anger.

As you will see on the anger thermometer in scenario one at the end of this chapter, research has shown that negative and/or irrational thoughts lend to escalating negative feelings. As scenario two (see page 369) shows, these negative feelings are associated with physiological changes such as tense muscles and headaches which in turn lead to dysregulation, ineffective parenting behaviors and poor consequences for children. The idea is to learn to cope with these emotional responses in a way that provides more self-control. First of all pay attention to your thoughts and feelings. If you find you are anxious, worrying with negative self-talk, stressing out and feeling guilty about your toddler's misbehavior, try to stop and challenge these thoughts – they won't help

you and aren't productive solutions. First of all remember that it is highly likely that your situation with your toddler is normal and has happened at one time or another to most other parents. You might say to yourself, "I'm stressed. That is natural. This feeling will pass." Indeed your feeling will pass, just as your toddler will eventually calm down. It just seems to take forever.

Second try to replace your upsetting

Don't let your negative feelings so overwhelm you that you are immobilized by inaction or lose control of your anger.

The important
message to
give yourself
and your
toddler is that
you can cope
calmly with
the situation.

**Give yourself
praise**

thoughts with alternative calming ones. For example, instead of thinking, "I can't handle this," or, "She never behaves. She is impossible," focus on your ability to use coping thoughts such as, "I can handle this, I can stay calm," or, "She needs me to be patient with her. It is better for my child see me take charge of my anger rather than let it control me," or, "She's just a toddler and can't control her responses." See Scenario #3 (page 370) for other positive thoughts you can use.

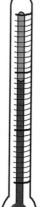

The important message to give yourself and your toddler is that you can cope calmly with the situation. Third, give yourself a pat on the back with self-praise for all your accomplishments as a parent. Examples of self-praising thoughts include, "I try hard," "I am learning about my child," and "I'm proud of myself for staying calm in the situation." Fourth, do some calm deep breathing and visualize a fun time you have had recently with your child, or read some of your positive self-praise thoughts in your journal on page 225) and make a positive prediction of a more relaxed future. Using this positive self-talk will result in you feeling calmer, more forgiving and understanding of your toddler's behavior and more able to problem solve some effecive solutions. Perhaps this will be a time to get some support, or take a break or use the ignore strategy and see the humor in the situation.

Teaching Toddlers How to Calm Down

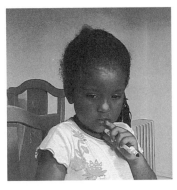

It is normal for toddlers to have difficulty self-regulating and learning to calm down. Parents can sometimes help their toddlers self-regulate by scaffolding with soothing words and physical cuddling. Sometimes a pacifier or special blanket or stuffed animal can help them self-soothe. And there will be times when nothing seems to work until the toddler works it through on his own. You can begin to help your toddler learn some rudimentary calm down strategies at times when your child is not actually upset. You can practice deep breathing with your toddler and help him see how it helps him to feel calm and relaxed. Here is a possible script for what to say to your toddler,

> *"Let's take a deep breath all the way down to our toes (wiggle your toes). Now let the breath slowly come out. Wow I'm feeling relaxed. Now let's do that again, deep breath pushed down to my toes..."*

Toddlers like to practice deep breathing by pretending to "Smell the flower. Now blow out a candle." This helps them breathe in through their noses and out through their mouths. It can be fun to practice this with a puppet. Perhaps your turtle puppet gets a little mad about something and then takes some deep breaths and goes in his shell and says, "I can calm down" and a little later comes out of his shell and says, "I feel calm now." Then the puppet and the child can practice this together. But remember, the toddler's main developmental milestones are of exploration, discovery and developing a sense of self. It is not until preschool age range that the developmental milestone of

There will be times when nothing seems to work until the toddler works it through on his own.

learning to self-regulate begins. So your efforts to teach your toddler to calm down will be primitive and don't expect the benefits for many years. Here are some key points for helping your toddler learn about calming down:

It is not until preschool age range that the developmental milestone of learning to self-regulate begins.

- When your child is calm, practice taking deep breaths and praise your child by telling him he is very strong at calming down.
- Notice times when your child stays calm in a frustrating situation and praise his patience and calmness.
- Use emotion coaching and comment on times your toddler is happy, excited, curious, calm, angry, or frustrated. Try to comment on more happy feelings than angry or sad ones.
- Model staying calm yourself in frustrating situations—take a deep breath—say, "I can calm down" in front of your child.

Certain Behaviors Should Not be Ignored

Ignoring is one of the most effective strategies you can use with toddlers when they throw tantrums—especially when ignoring is combined with distractions and praise for the opposite positive behaviors. However, some parents ignore all their children's misbehaviors, regardless of their severity or the setting in which they occur. This is not an appropriate approach for behaviors that are destructive to children themselves, other people or property. It is paramount that parents keep their own children as well as other children safe.

In most circumstances, annoying behaviors such as whining, pouting, screaming, spitting, and tantrums can be dealt with effectively by ignoring. On the other hand, dangerous or abusive behaviors, including hitting, running away, biting and damaging property must not be ignored. In addition, although it is not harmful to ignore avoidance behaviors (child keeps playing when you tell him it's time to wash his hands), if you ignore your child when he is not following your commands, you are not likely to get the response you want. Therefore, it's important to select the behaviors you are going to ignore with care and to remember that ignoring an inappropriate behavior will only be effective with those for which parental attention is the primary reinforcement.

Abusive behaviors, including hitting, verbal abuse, running away, biting and damaging property must not be ignored.

Examples of Behaviors That Can be Effectively Ignored in Toddlers

- Whining, pouting
- Temper tantrums
- Facial grimaces
- Minor squabbles
- Crying
- Picky or messy eating
- Protests when prohibited from doing or having something
- Nose picking
- Messy pants (ignore mess while changing child's pants)
- Thumb sucking
- Baby talk (done for effect when your child is capable of more grown up talk)

**Ignore select
behaviors**

Pay Attention to Positive Opposite Behaviors

Some parents become so engrossed in their own activities that they fail to pay attention when their children speak nicely, share toys, eat with a spoon, or play quietly. If these positive behaviors are ignored, they will disappear. Parents often develop a reflex response, reacting to their children only when they get into trouble. This negative cycle of paying attention when toddlers misbehave and ignoring them when they are behaving appropriately actually strengthens these neural connections and increases the frequency of misbehavior.

If you use ignoring, it is crucial that you give attention and praise to positive behaviors, particularly those that are the opposite of the one you are ignoring. We call this praising the "positive opposite." If you've decided to ignore whining, for instance, you should make a conscious effort to praise your child whenever he speaks politely. You might say, "I really like it when you use your polite voice." If you're concerned that your child is grabbing and hitting, you need to praise him for sharing and keeping his hands to his own body.

TODDLER ALERT

Official Time Out procedures where a child is expected to sit quietly in a chair for two to three minutes are not started until children are over three years old and have developed more self-control and the regulatory ability to be able to sit in a specific place.

Time Away for Hitting and Biting

Hitting or biting are not behaviors you can ignore because someone may be hurt.

Most toddlers bite or hit other children when they are frustrated. This is not a behavior you can ignore because someone may be hurt. A parent can respond with a firm command, "no biting," coupled with quickly separating the children temporarily so the biter doesn't continue to hurt the other child. The child who has been hit or bitten may be coached with words to tell her friend, "I don't like that" and the biter removed to another part of the room. After a brief separation (one to two minutes) during which the biter is ignored, he is then redirected to a new activity. In essence this extended ignore procedure gives the child a chance to calm down, avoids giving attention for the misbehavior, and keeps the other child safe from being hurt.

Some strategies for coping with biting

If toddler bites another child:
- Separate the children immediately
- Kind, but firm, limit setting - "no biting"
- Stay calm
- Help child who was bitten to say, "I don't like that" to the child who bit him
- If possible, provide child with words to resolve the conflict that led to the biting.
  For example, "looks like you want a truck too, you can say, "I want a truck, please." (Even if the child can't say these words, the parent will still have modeled a better coping strategy.)

My responses are firm

If toddler bites parent:
- Parent stays calm, even though the bite may startle and hurt
- Kind but firm limit setting "no biting" and briefly put child down or move away just a foot or two
- Tell child that the biting hurt
- Redirect and reengage child in a new activity, or provide them with words to communicate the reason for the bite. For example, "I know you don't want to have your diaper changed, I'm sorry. You can bring your blue dog while we do it."

Biting behavior often causes parents or daycare teachers to overreact but is actually quite common between 15 months and three years of age. With the emergence of language skills, biting and hitting subsides for most children because they have another way of expressing their needs or frustrations.

TODDLER ALERT

Sometimes parents may bite children back or wash their mouths out with soap or Tabasco sauce to stop them from biting. Neither of these parental responses will work in the long run, and instead this will model an aggressive and hurtful response. Remember that the way your toddler learns best is by watching you, so if you use a hurtful or aggressive discipline technique (biting back), your toddler will learn that biting is an acceptable way of dealing with frustration.

Brief ignores—"Differential Attention"

In the next scenario we will see how a father sets limits and uses his attention and ignoring to dress his 18-month-old daughter.

Father is dressing his daughter Lia and says, "Stand calmly on the ground." She jumps up and down and Father repeats his request, "Stand calmly on the ground." When she doesn't stand still he turns his head away and ignores her, and when she stops jumping he turns back to her saying, "Thank you, good standing still." She starts jumping again and he turns his head away to ignore again. He repeats his request and when she stops jumping again he turns back to her, rubs her back, kisses and says, "I like the way you stand still. Thank you." He starts putting on her shirt and reminds her, "Stand still." She puts in one arm and Father praises her, "Good for you getting your arm in. That is hard work." She has some frustration with getting her second arm in and father says, "Lia, I need you to be calm." She jumps briefly and Father makes no comment and then she continues to try to get her arm in the sleeve, and Father says, "You are trying so hard to get your hand out." He cheers when she gets her hand through the sleeve.

Dressing often becomes a battle for 18 months to two-year-olds.

This is a good example of "differential attention;" that is, giving attention to the calm behavior as soon as it occurs while ignoring the jumping and uncooperative behavior. Dressing often becomes a battle for 18-months-to two-year-olds. Parents can find strategies to make this easier such as easier clothing, giving the toddler something to hold while the parent dresses him, turning dressing into a game, inviting the toddler's input into what he will put on first and so forth.

Parents Finding Support

It is often very difficult for parents to control their anger when they are confronted with children's aggression, noncompliance, and constant whining. In many cases it may seem as though the child is misbehaving on purpose in an attempt to "get your goat." Try to refrain from making attributions about the child's intentions or interpreting the inappropriate behavior as a personal attack. Remember that the toddler's developmental task is to explore and to establish some independence. This drive will conflict with parents' efforts to put limits on their behavior. In addition, toddlers' limited language skills and lack of ability to self-regulate makes it hard for them to use more appropriate social behaviors. Dysregulated behavior is normal for this age group, and it is the parents' responsibility to socialize or teach their children to use more appropriate strategies to get what they want.

The key is always to stay calm as possible and avoid showing signs of distress or anger. Being confronted by an angry parent can be a frightening experience for a child and can serve to ratchet up the child's own emotional state. Try to view your child's inappropriate behavior as objectively as possible, because your own emotional involvement will cloud the issue. Remember, the issue is the occurrence of the negative behavior, and the goal is to respond to the behavior in a way that will reduce the intensity and frequency of the misbehavior and promote the positive opposite desired behavior. Of course, this is easier said than done, and all parents lose their temper sometimes. Try to find ways to get the support and relaxation that you need. Take time for yourself and develop a support team from family and friends. Find ways to have some time away from your toddler and engage in activities that are calming or rejuvenating to you: exercise, get a massage, go shopping, socialize with friends, or watch a movie. While the toddler years may seem overwhelming at times, they will pass quickly and your toddler will soon be a verbal and somewhat more reasonable preschooler.

Find ways to have some time away from your toddler and engage in activities that are calming or rejuvenating to you.

To Sum Up...

If you decide to use ignoring, you must be determined to see the ignoring through until the misbehavior stops. Consistency is the essence of ignoring. When your child throws a tantrum, you may be tempted to give in. However, each time you do so you actually make the misbehavior worse because you teach him that he can outlast you. The next time, the tantrum will be louder and last longer. Therefore, you must continue ignoring until the behavior changes.

Remember that ignoring is only effective if you and your child have a strong initial bond. Ignoring works because your child craves and values your attention. Therefore, the first task in any plan to change behavior is to increase your attention, toddler-directed play, coaching, and praise for positive behaviors. Although ignoring will decrease annoying misbehaviors, it will not increase positive ones. To do this, it must be combined with social approval for prosocial behaviors as well as teaching and modeling positive social behaviors and positive emotional language in your interactions with your children.

Points to Remember about
POSITIVE DISCIPLINE HELPS MY TODDLER FEEL LOVED AND SECURE

- Play frequently and provide social and emotional coaching
- Label and reflect your toddler's feelings; noticing both positive and negative feelings
- Structure your toddler's day with a predictable routine for mornings, naps, meals, and bedtime
- Set clear limits when needed to keep your toddler safe
- Help your toddler prepare for transitions or changes in routine
- Have a predictable routine for leaving your child and reuniting
- Give your toddler choices when possible
- Share your love and praise and tell your toddler how special he is
- Give your toddler attention and praise for positive behavior
- Redirect your toddler's negative behavior
- Allow your toddler independence when possible
- Help your toddler explore while giving appropriate support and monitoring
- Ignore tantrums and give back attention as soon as tantrum stops
- Take care of yourself by getting support from others and doing things for yourself

Points to Remember about
IGNORING

- Avoid eye contact and discussion while ignoring
- Physically move away from your child but stay in the room
- Be prepared for testing
- Be consistent
- Return your attention as soon as misbehavior stops
- Combine distractions and redirections with ignoring
- Choose specific child behaviors to ignore and make sure they are ones you can ignore and keep your child safe
- Limit the number of behaviors to systematically ignore
- Give more attention to the positive opposite behaviors you want to encourage

**Be prepared
for testing**

Points to Remember about
MANAGING BITING AND HITTING

If your child bites or hits another child:

• Separate the children immediately.
• Use kind but firm limit setting "no biting," "no hitting."
• Stay calm.
• Help child who was bitten or hit to say "I don't like that."

I can redirect and re-engage my child

• If possible, provide your child with words to resolve the conflict that led to the biting or hitting; e.g., "Looks like you want a truck too, you can say, 'I want a truck, please.'" (Even if your child can't say these words, you have still modeled a better coping strategy.)

If your child bites or hits you:

• Do your best to stay calm, even though the bite or hit may startle you and hurt.
• Use kind but firm limit setting, "no biting" and briefly put your child down or move away just a foot or two.
• Tell your child that the biting hurt.
• Ignore child for 1–2 minutes.
• Redirect and reengage your child in a new activity, or provide her with words to communicate the reason for the bite.

Points to Remember about
HANDLING TANTRUM STORMS

Daily tantrums are a normal part of the toddler years. They occur because developmentally toddlers lack the verbal skills to communicate their feelings or wants, and have an immature emotional self-regulation system. This, coupled with a strong drive to explore and be independent, is a recipe for frustration for your toddler.

• Stay calm in the face of your toddler's storm—including kicking, screaming, throwing things or hitting.
• Don't try to reason or use a distraction with your toddler in the middle of a storm—the more you reason, comfort, or yell, the worse the storm will rage.
• Stay in the room with your toddler while the storm occurs, but ignore the tantrum; do something else.
• Wait for the storm to subside and then return your attention immediately; praise your child's calm behavior and distract him to some other activity.
• No matter how long the storm lasts, don't give in or negotiate—even when you are in public. This short-term solution will lead to longer-term consequences of escalating tantrums and using these to get what he wants.
• Stay calm and in control—a tantrumming child is feeling out of control and needs to feel that his parent is in control.

**Stay calm
and in control**

• If your toddler's tantrum escalates to hitting people or pets, or breaking objects, pick him up and carry him to a safe place. Then stay with him but ignore the tantrum.
• Think about why your child might be tantrumming.
• Try to pre-empt storms when possible.

Think about why and when your child's tantrums occur—is it when your child is hungry? Or, tired? Or, involved in a transition to some other activity? Or, can't have something s/he wants? This might mean keeping snacks on hand, setting an earlier nap time, or preparing your child in advance for a transition to give him a chance to adjust. If your child is grappling with control or independence issues, try offering choices when possible. Monitor how often you are saying "no." Are your limits necessary? Save your battles for the important issues.

Points to Remember about
STAYING CALM & RESPECTFUL

When you first start ignoring misbehavior, the behavior will get worse before it gets better. It is important to stay calm while ignoring. Try to think ahead, brainstorm and remain calm when ignoring misbehavior.

Some Examples of Ways to Stay Calm While Ignoring
deep breaths
relaxation techniques
positive thoughts
walk away
turn on some music
put angry thoughts in parking lot!

Remember, all young children cry, bite and hit to get what they want. This is not personal but a reflection of their lack of verbal skills and inability to use social skills to get what they want.

Points to Remember about
PUTTING IT ALL TOGETHER

1. Identify and label your thoughts and emotions when they first occur. Pay attention to how your body feels (for example, tenseness, fidgeting, anger, headaches).
2. Decide what events make you feel frustrated.
3. Choose the most effective way to control yourself, and do it.
4. Make a positive action plan.

Non-constructive Thoughts

"He's doing this on purpose."

"When will he ever learn—we do this every day and it's still a battle."

"I'm really horrible for feeling so angry. I bet other parents don't lose their tempers."

Constructive Thoughts

"He's tired and hungry. That's why he's so irritable."

"He's trying to exert his independence. It must be hard to have to get dressed every morning when he wants to do it alone, but doesn't have the skills."

"I can handle this. I can stay in control. He's just testing the limits. My job is to stay calm and help him learn better ways."

I use coping thoughts

SCENARIO #1: ANGER THERMOMETER
Negative Irrational Thoughts lead to Negative Feelings

NEGATIVE THOUGHTS
I'm so mad I could scream…
S/he deserves to be…
S/he is no good/rotten.
What did I do to deserve…
It's not my fault; it's his/hers.
S/he's just like…
I was never like this.
I don't have time to deal with this.
I'm a bad parent (partner). I'm hopeless
Why me? This is too stressful.
It's not working to stay calm.
It's useless…
There's no point in doing anything for him/her.
It never helps.
No matter what I do, nothing stops her crying.
I deserve this for what I did when…
My parents told me I was…(a criticism)
What's going to happen when s/he's a teenager?
Maybe this is too much for me to handle.
Maybe I'm not a good parent/spouse.
I'm not sure I can control this.

NEGATIVE FEELINGS
Furious
Contemptuous
Angry
Impatient
Hostile
Defensive
Guilt
Withdrawn
Frustrated
Depressed
Inadequate
Resentful
Irritated
Anxious
Worried
Helpless

SCENARIO #2: ESCALATING NEGATIVE OUTCOMES
Negative Feelings lead to Ineffective Behavior and Consequences

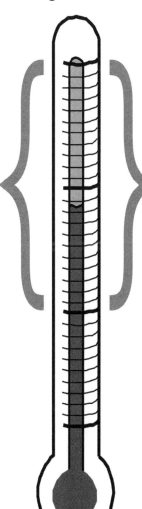

NEGATIVE FEELINGS

Furious
Contemptuous
Angry
Impatience
Hostile
Defensive Guilt
Withdrawn
Frustrated
Depression
Irritated
Anxious
Worried

PHYSIOLOGICAL SIGNS

Heart racing
Neck muscles tight
Chest Tight
Clenched fists
Teeth clenched
Headache
Shallow rapid
   breathing
Increased
   perspiration
Muscles tense
Pacing
Headache
   developing

INEFFECTIVE BEHAVIOR, ACTIONS AND MODELING

Yelling
Hitting
Threatening
Withdrawing
   fom others
Neglect
Criticizing
Difficulty listening
Thinking narrow
Less open to
   new ideas

SCENARIO #3: CALM DOWN THERMOMETER
Positive Coping Thoughts lead to Positive Feelings and Effective Parenting

POSITIVE THOUGHTS

Toddler compliance gets better 3-4 years of age.

I can make a difference to my toddler's emotional development.

I can handle this; I can control my anger.

She needs me to be patient with her.

His/her positive qualities are…

I'm a caring parent/partner because I'm trying by…

I stay calm most of the time.

I enjoy being with him/her, especially when we…

I love (appreciate)…

Toddlers are supposed to be curious and discover.

FEELINGS

Alert/ Interested

Calm

Happy

Confident

Content

Loving/ Affectionate

Compassionate

POSITIVE ACTIONS

Calm

Positive parenting

Self care

SCENARIO #3: CALM DOWN THERMOMETER
Positive Coping Thoughts lead to Positive Feelings and Effective Parenting

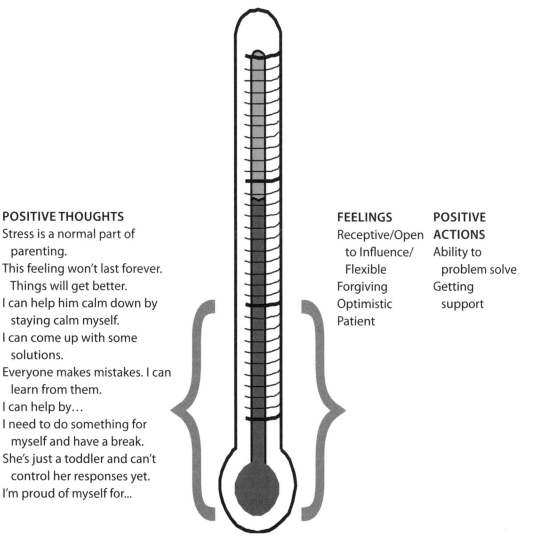

POSITIVE THOUGHTS

Stress is a normal part of parenting.

This feeling won't last forever. Things will get better.

I can help him calm down by staying calm myself.

I can come up with some solutions.

Everyone makes mistakes. I can learn from them.

I can help by…

I need to do something for myself and have a break.

She's just a toddler and can't control her responses yet.

I'm proud of myself for...

FEELINGS

Receptive/Open to Influence/ Flexible

Forgiving

Optimistic

Patient

POSITIVE ACTIONS

Ability to problem solve

Getting support

Parents' Viewpoint
MY IGNORING JOURNAL

Behaviors such as throwing tantrums, whining, pouting, sulking, and screaming, are good candidates for ignoring. These behaviors are annoying, but they never really seem to hurt anyone, and the behaviors will disappear if they are systematically ignored. The ignoring technique should not be used, however, with behaviors that could lead to physical injury or property damage, or intolerable disruption of an ongoing activity. Ignoring is one of the most effective strategies you can use for behaviors such as whining and crying.

Child Behaviors I will Ignore
e.g., whining

Goal:
I will commit to ignoring_____behavior whenever it occurs.

I will praise_____behavior, the positive opposite of the behavior I am ignoring.

Parents' Viewpoint
USING DIFFERENTIAL ATTENTION JOURNAL

Sometimes, children will show positive and negative behaviors during the same activity. For example, a child might follow directions (positive behavior) while whining or fussing (negative behavior). Differential attention is the technique where a parent praises the positive behavior while ignoring the negative behavior. For example, a parent might praise the child for following directions, and pay no attention to the whining or fussing behavior. This way, the child learns that she will receive positive attention for some behaviors, but will not receive attention for other behavior (e.g., whining).

When Would Differential Attention be Effective?
e.g., when child is following directions and fussing at the same time, praise his cooperation and ignore his fussing.

Goal: I will commit to praising _____ behavior while ignoring

_____ behavior.

POSITIVE OPPOSITES BEHAVIOR JOURNAL

Plan to give more attention to positive opposite behavior while ignoring the negative behavior. Remember to keep building your parent pyramid foundation of using persistence, social and emotion coaching, praise, giving choices and using redirections and distractions.

Behaviors I want to see less of: e.g., hitting	**For each negative behavior, put its positive opposite behavior below:** e.g., staying calm and using words
1.	1.
2.	2.
3.	3.
4.	4.
5.	5.
6.	6.
7.	7.
8.	8.

Parents' Viewpoint
MY CALM DOWN JOURNAL

Write down here some strategies you will use to stay calm when ignoring or getting frustrated with your toddler's behavior.

Ways I will stay calm:

Goal:

I will commit to tell myself the following when I am getting frustrated:

_____

Parents' Viewpoint
SELF-TALK IN PROBLEM SITUATION

Identify a problem situation and the upsetting thoughts you have at the time. Write down some alternative calming thoughts that you might use to redefine the situation. Next time you find yourself using negative self-talk, give yourself some time to think positively and consider the alternative thoughts available to you thinking about the situation.

Problem Situation | **Upsetting Thoughts** | **Calming Thoughts**

Positive Actions

MY TODDLER'S PICTURE
(30-36 months)

CHAPTER 8

Summary–
Putting it all Together

In order to cope with the inevitable frustrations of parenting, it is important that parents find support from their partners or friends or other parents and family members. It is also important to find ways to refuel your energy so you can stay consistent and predictable in your responses.

In this book we have talked about promoting your child's language, social, and emotional brain development as well as strengthening her positive attachment and trust in you. We have focused on balancing the toddler's need for exploration and independence with safety and necessary limit setting. Let's review a few of the principles we have discussed:

- Be warm, positive, and loving; show your children you enjoy them.
- Use academic, social and emotion coaching strategies during toddler-directed play times. This coaching will teach your child how to be friendly and how to communicate.

- Model and be respectful in your interactions with your child—this will teach her to be respectful with you.
- Think about your child's developmental needs and temperament. Be patient and adjust your expectations accordingly.
- Structure your toddler's day with predictable routines for bedtime, morning time, meals, separations and reunions.
- Use redirections, distractions, and choices to preempt misbehavior; avoid too may commands and "no's."
- Withdraw your attention and ignore misbehaviors that are not hurtful to others or to themselves.
- Set clear limits when needed to keep your toddler safe.
- Use a brief time away for aggressive behavior such as biting, hitting or destructing objects.
- Praise your child's positive behavior often.
- Provide constant supervision and a safe environment.
- Be patient and stay calm. Remember toddlers are striving to explore and are not misbehaving deliberately.
- Use positive coping thoughts, self-care strategies, and develop a parent support team so your own emotional bank account is full and you can continue to nurture your toddler.

Use predictable routines

Parents' Viewpoint
PARENTS THINKING LIKE DETECTIVES: SEE WHAT YOU'VE LEARNED

To review what you have learned from reading this book, make a list of what strategies you would use for the following toddler behaviors.

Problem Behavior	Positive Parenting Strategy
1. Hitting peers	_____
2. Refusing to do what parent asks	_____
3. Biting others	_____
4. Dawdling	_____
5. Picky eating	_____
6. Aggressive with animals	_____
7. Throwing tantrums	_____
8. Soiling pants	_____
9. Stomach aches and headaches	_____
10. Inattentiveness and impulsivity	_____
11. Wetting bed at night	_____

Problem Behavior	Positive Parenting Strategy
12. Running away in grocery store	
13. Refusing to sit in car seat	
14. Crying when left in child care	
15. Refusing to share toy with peer	
16. Not sitting at dinner table	
17. Watching too much TV	
18. Getting into parents' bed at night	
19. Refusing to go to bed at bedtime	
20. Taking a toy from a peer	
21. Throwing food on the floor	
22. Crying, whining	

Add other problem behaviors you are wanting to manage on this list and decide on the appropriate parenting discipline response.

Problem Behavior	Positive Parenting Strategy

I use effective parenting responses

Problem Behavior   **Positive Parenting Strategy**

_____   _____

_____   _____

_____   _____

_____   _____

_____   _____

_____   _____

_____   _____

_____   _____

_____   _____

_____   _____

Incredible Years Problem Solving Worksheet
FOR MANAGING TODDLERS' CHALLENGING BEHAVIOR

Here is worksheet for you to reflect on all the parenting strategies you are going to use to manage a challenging misbehavior while at the same time teaching him the replacement behavior. Fill out this form and make a date to review again to see if you have been successful at reducing this misbehavior.

Problem Definition

1. My child's challenging behavior:

2. What are the triggers/precipitants of my child's misbehavior? (developmental problem, not enough sleep, not getting what he wants, a family transition or stress, low frustration tolerance, divorce etc.)

3. How do I usually respond to this misbehavior? (Do I give it attention? Do I get angry?)

Goals:

4. What is my goal? What positive opposite behavior do I want to see instead?

Solutions:

5. What skills/strategies can I use from the bottom of the Parenting Pyramid to support this positive behavior?

What kind of play might best help my child here? (Remember, it is best if it is child-led.) (persistence, academic, social, or emotion coaching)

Praise: What behaviors can I praise and how? (Remember they should be the "positive opposites" of the behaviors you want to decrease.)

6. Choose from the list below those responses from the top of
   the pyramid that can be used to reduce this misbehavior.

   Routines: Do I have a predictable routine for this problem?

   Distraction/Redirection: How can I distract or redirect my child
   before misbehavior escalates?

   Ignore: What part of this behavior could I ignore?

   What will I say to myself while I ignore it?

   Calm Down Strategies: What calm down strategies can I teach my
   child? (use of turtle shell, deep breathing, positive self-talk "I can do it, I
   can calm down," use of the calm-down thermometer)

Carrying Out my Plan:

7. To whom should I communicate this plan? (teachers, grandparents, partners, etc.)

8. Who can I call for support and to check in?

9. How will I take care of myself while this is going on?

Evaluating the Success of My Solutions

10. How will I know I am making progress? What will be different?

11. How will I celebrate my child's success? As well as my own?

Remember it can take three weeks or more to see changes, so don't give up!

Parents' Viewpoint
THINGS I'VE ENJOYED MOST IN PARENTING MY TODDLER

Parents' Viewpoint
THINGS I'VE ENJOYED MOST IN PARENTING MY TODDLER

MY TODDLER'S PICTURE

LETTER TO MY TODDLER

Write a letter here about your thoughts, feelings and hopes for your toddler's future.

Dear _____,

Research Studies and Materials Regarding Incredible Years Programs

Research articles and studies regarding the Incredible Years programs can be found on the Incredible Years web site, www.incredibleyears.com. The following chapter reference reviews Incredible Years research followed by some other Incredible Years books for parents, teachers and children.

Review of Research

Webster-Stratton, C., & Reid, M. J. (2010). *The Incredible Years Parents, Teachers and Children Training Series: A multifaceted treatment approach for young children with conduct problems.* In J. Weisz & A. Kazdin (Eds.), Evidence-based psychotherapies for children and adolescents, 2nd edition (pp. 194-210). New York: Guilford Publications.

Incredible Years Teacher Books

Webster-Stratton, C. (1999). *How to promote children's social and emotional competence.* London: Sage Publications.

Incredible Years Parent Book

Webster-Stratton, C. (2006). *The Incredible Years: A trouble-shooting guide for parents of children ages 3-8 years.* Seattle: Incredible Years Press.

Webster-Stratton, C. (2011). *Incredible Babies: A Guide and Journal of Your Baby's First Year—Ways to Promote Your Baby's Social, Emotional and Language Development.* Seattle: Incredible Years Press.

Incredible Years Children's Books about Anger Management, Social Skills and Problem Solving

Webster-Stratton, C. (1998). *Wally's Detective Book for Solving Problems at School.* Seattle, WA: Incredible Years Press.

Webster-Stratton, C. (1998). *Wally's Detective Book for Solving Problems at Home.* Seattle, WA: Incredible Years Press.

Webster-Stratton, C. (1998). *Wally Learns a Lesson from Tiny Turtle.* Seattle, WA: Incredible Years Press.

Webster-Stratton, C. (1998). *Wally Meets Dina Dinosaur.* Seattle, WA: Incredible Years Press.

Some Classic References

There are thousands of articles and books related to child development, temperament, parenting and children's learning. The reader is referred to the internet for such materials. Here are a few of my favorite classics regarding the underlying theory of cognitive and behavior learning and child development.

Cognitive Development Classics

Inhelder, B. and J. Piaget (1958). *The Growth of Logical Thinking from Childhood to Adolescence.* New York: Basic Books.

Piaget, J. (1962). *Play, Dreams and Imitation in Childhood.* New York: Norton.

Piaget, J., and Inhelder, B. (1962). *The Psychology of the Child.* New York: Basic Books.

Piaget, J. (1951). *The Psychology of Intelligence.* London: Routledge and Kegan Paul.

Rizzolatti G & Craighero L (2004) The mirror-neuron system *Ann Rev Neurosci* 27: 169–192.

Schwartz, R. & Garaoni, G. (1989). Cognitive balance and psychopathology: Evaluation of an information processing model of positive and negative states of mind, Clinical Psychology Review, 9, 271-294.

Development Classics

Ames, L. B. et. al., (1979) *The Gesell Institute's Child from One to Six.* New York: Harper and Row.

Chess, S. & Thomas, A. (1987) *Know Your Child.* New York: Basic Books.

Thomas, Chess & Birch (1968). *Temperament and Behavior Disorders in Children.* New York, New York University Press.

See http://www.cdc.gov/ncbddd/child/toddlers2.htm

Language Development

Fernald, Anne. (1985) Four-month-old Infants Prefer to Listen to Motherese *Infant Behav & Dev* 8: 303-306.

Gopnik, A., Meltzoff, A. N., & Kuhl, P. K. (1999). *The Scientist in the Crib.* Perennial Publishers.

Hart B & Risley TR. (1992) American parenting of language-learning children: persisting differences in family-child interactions observed in natural home environments. *Dev Psychol.* 28:1096–1105.

Modeling Theory and Social Learning

Bandura, A. (1977) *Social Learning Theory.* New York, General Learning Press.

Committee on Public Education (2001) Children, Adolescents and television *Pediatrics* 107(2): 423 – 426.

Bandura, A (1965) Influence of model's reinforcement contingencies on the acquisition of imitated responses *J. Person & Soc Psych* 1: 589 – 595.

Bandura, A (2006) Toward a psychology of human agency *Persp Psych Sci* 1: 164– 180.

Patterson Patterson, G. R. (1975a). Families: Applications of social learning to family life. Champaign, IL: Research Press.

Patterson, G. R. (1980). Mothers: the unacknowledged victims. Monograms for the Society For Research in Child Development, 186(5), 1-64.

Patterson, G. R. (1982). Coercive family process. Eugene, OR: Castalia.

Reading

Codell, E. R. (2003). *How to Get Your Child to Love Reading.* New York: Workman Publishing.

Research on TV viewing

Zimmerman, F. J., & Christakis, D. A. (2005). Children's television viewing and cognitive outcomes *Pediatrics* 159, 619-625.

Zimmerman F.J. et al (2007). Associations between media viewing and language Development in Children under Age 2 Years *Journal of Pediatrics* 151: 364 – 369.